A FEW
GREAT
SCIENTISTS

A FEW GREAT SCIENTISTS

FROM ALFRED NOBEL TO CARL SAGAN

JORGE ALBERTO DELUCCA

Copyright © 2017 by Jorge Alberto Delucca.

Library of Congress Control Number: 2017911587
ISBN: Hardcover 978-1-5434-3931-1
Softcover 978-1-5434-3930-4
eBook 978-1-5434-4013-3

All rights reserved. No part of this book may be reproduced or transmitted in any form or by any means, electronic or mechanical, including photocopying, recording, or by any information storage and retrieval system, without permission in writing from the copyright owner.

Any people depicted in stock imagery provided by Thinkstock are models, and such images are being used for illustrative purposes only.
Certain stock imagery © Thinkstock.

Print information available on the last page.

Rev. date: 07/25/2017

To order additional copies of this book, contact:
Xlibris
1-888-795-4274
www.Xlibris.com
Orders@Xlibris.com

CONTENTS

INTRODUCTION VII
to a Few Great Scientists

ALFRED NOBEL 1
The King of Dynamite

JOHN VON NEUMANN 29
Mathematical Genius

JONAS SALK 49
The Man Who Conquered Polio

WATSON AND CRICK 59
The Search for the Double Helix

RACHEL CARSON 71
Mother of the Environmental Movement

NORMAN BORLAUG 87
and His Army of Hunger Fighters

RICHARD FEYNMAN 111
Physicist, Genius, and a Very Funny Curious Character

CARL SAGAN 133
Adventures in the Cosmos

REFERENCE LIST 161

Introduction
to a Few Great Scientists
From Alfred Nobel to Carl Sagan

I grew up during the 1960s, an era where the heroes in so many TV movies and comic books were scientists. Many schoolchildren, including me, dreamed of becoming scientists. Sometime during high school, I decided to be a nuclear physicist; and when I entered college, I enrolled in the College of Arts and Sciences at the University of Puerto Rico–Mayaguez, planning to major in physics. One day, my father asked me if I was studying engineering. When I said physics, he warned me that there would not be many professional opportunities for me as a physicist and advised me to major in engineering. Wisely, I listened and transferred to chemical engineering. I graduated in 1976, and I also commissioned as an officer in the US Air Force. My first job in the air force was as an intercontinental ballistic missile officer where I was working with nuclear weapons. After four years, I had the opportunity to transfer into the bioenvironmental engineering career field, a mix of environmental engineering, radiation safety officer, and industrial hygienist. I graduated from the bioenvironmental engineering course at the USAF School of Aerospace Medicine at Brooks AFB in San Antonio, Texas, in 1982. The job awoke my old taste for science, and I enjoyed the mathematics used to solve practical problems. I was finally using science to prevent problems of pollution and to protect people from exposure to toxic substances. Eventually, I completed a master's degree of science in environmental management from the University of Oklahoma. A few years later, I had the honor of teaching environmental science at the University of Phoenix–Oklahoma City.

As a teenager, I developed a passion for reading. One book I read as a fourteen-year-old was *Microbe Hunters* by Paul de Kruif. Years later, I bought a copy of the book and reread it. I admired the simple, easy-to-read, and upbeat style of this book. Through the years, I read many award-winning history books, but I felt that often the authors spent too much time on small details. I decided that if I ever wrote a book, it would be in a similar style as *Microbe Hunters*.

For years, I debated what to write about. I loved history and felt that I did not have enough patience for fiction. But I admired scientists and still felt some frustration at not being able to have been a "true scientist." So what was the compromise? I could write about scientists. But there were so many scientists! I had to write about a few of them. My knowledge of marketing from my master's degree in business administration taught me that to be successful, you need to do something that many people will be interested in. So I should write about scientists that people recognized and would like to know more about. So I picked a short list of some of the most fascinating scientists in modern times. I chose to start with Alfred Nobel, a chemist, who found practical and peaceful applications for nitroglycerin and later invented dynamite. The story of why he conceived the idea of the Nobel prizes is something that most people do not know and will make fascinating reading. Although he lived in the nineteenth century, his Nobel prizes and Nobel laureates have a great influence in modern times, so I feel that my decision to start this book with him is well justified. I hope that the readers agree and enjoy my selection of scientists and the stories of their achievements.

Jorge Alberto Delucca
Moore, Oklahoma
December 27, 2015

Alfred Nobel
The King of Dynamite

> My dynamite will sooner lead to peace than a thousand world conventions. As soon as men will find that in one instant, whole armies can be utterly destroyed, they will abide by golden peace.
> —Alfred Nobel

Alfred Nobel was not a research scientist like the other scientists I discuss in the other chapters of this book. Although he was educated as a chemist, he found applications in construction for nitroglycerin and, later, for his invention: dynamite. The Swedish government referred to him in official documents as a "civil engineer." But he owned several industrial plants to manufacture nitroglycerin and dynamite, and for that, he also qualifies as a chemical engineer. But you and I will refer to him as an industrial chemist and, therefore, an applied scientist. Alfred worked intensely in his various laboratories. He focused on the development of explosives technology and other chemical inventions, such as synthetic rubber and leather and artificial silks among others. By the time of his death in 1896, he had 355 patents.

Nitroglycerin was not discovered by Alfred Nobel but by an Italian chemist called Ascanio Sobrero. Sobrero noticed that, if he placed a drop on a hard surface and hit it with a hammer, it would explode. It was fun, but he had no idea what to do with this substance. Nitroglycerin was considered to be too dangerous to be of any practical use since it would explode if subjected to heat or pressure. But it was far more powerful than gunpowder. Alfred Nobel took this discovery and made it one of the scientific discoveries that changed history.

Alfred Bernhard Nobel was born on October 21, 1833, in Stockholm, Sweden. His father, Immanuel Nobel, was an engineer, industrialist, and inventor. His mother was Caroline Andrietta Ahlsell. Alfred was a direct descendant of Olof Rudbeck, a medical pioneer who investigated the lymphatic system.

Alfred's father worked as an engineer in the construction of railroads and bridges and searched for ways to blast rock more efficiently. Immanuel's construction business in Russia failed the year Alfred was born. He moved his family to Stockholm. Four years later, he moved to Russia and opened a factory in Saint Petersburg to supply armaments to the Russian military. He developed naval mines that successfully protected the port from invasion by the British navy during the Crimean War.

In 1842, Immanuel moved his family to Saint Petersburg where Alfred was educated by tutors and became fluent in Swedish, Russian, French, English, and German by age seventeen. He was primarily interested in literature and poetry, as well as chemistry and physics. His father wanted Alfred and his brothers to join him in his business as engineers. He did not approve of Alfred's interest in poetry and literature and sent him abroad to study chemistry. In 1850, Alfred was sent to Paris where he studied under the famous chemist Théophile-Jules Pelouze at the University of Torino. There, Alfred met Pelouze's assistant, the Italian chemist Ascanio Sobrero, who invented nitroglycerin. By 1849, Alfred was a trained chemist. He was a brilliant student who had done extensive studies of his own, and his laboratory skills were vastly superior to those of his two older brothers, Robert and Ludvig, and his contemporaries. Immanuel was a good inventor and entrepreneur but not as good a businessman. Alfred and his brothers proved to be much better inventors and businessmen than their father. In 1856, when the Crimean War ended and Czar Alexander II had to sign a humiliating peace treaty, the Russian government stopped purchasing armaments from Nobel and sons. Immanuel was threatened by bankruptcy for the second time in his career. Ludvig was able to liquidate the family enterprise and guaranteed a small sum of money to start over in Stockholm. Alfred set up a laboratory, started developing inventions such as a gasometer—an apparatus for measuring liquids—and a manometer for measuring pressure, and obtained patents. But none of those inventions resulted in a good source of income. Alfred got in touch with his former professor of chemistry and learned about Ascano Sobrero's nitroglycerin. Sobrero warned about trying to find any use for the nitroglycerin, which he considered to be too volatile and dangerous. But Alfred was fascinated by it. The challenge for Alfred was how to detonate and liberate the awesome power of this substance. After a number of experiments, Alfred conceived the idea of mixing nitroglycerin with gunpowder and lighting the mixture with a regular fuse. With Robert and Ludvig, he executed several successful explosions on the frozen Neva River outside Saint Petersburg.

Alfred wrote his father about his successes with the new explosive, and his father started experimenting on his own. But when Immanuel wrote Alfred about the great results he was getting in his experiments, Alfred became concerned that his father was jumping to conclusions. Alfred travelled to Stockholm and found that, as he suspected, his father was using faulty measuring methods leading to exaggerated results. After an argument between Alfred and Immanuel, the latter claimed that the idea of mixing nitroglycerin with gunpowder was his own. Alfred left for Saint Petersburg in a fit of anger. Upon his arrival at Saint Petersburg, he wrote a letter to his father, explaining Immanuel's technical errors. This was one of several episodes of tension between Alfred and Immanuel. Alfred wrote: "It should not seem strange that I, at the age of thirty, will not allow myself to be treated as a school boy." But there was no breach between him and his father, and the letter appears to have cleared the air between them.

After the anger subsided, Alfred, Immanuel, and young Emil began experimenting with gunpowder and nitroglycerin. They received a grant from the military for a demonstration at Karlsborg's fortress. Alfred loaded a pig-iron bomb with half gunpowder and half nitroglycerin. But when the bomb exploded, it was so powerful that even the military officers were frightened.

The military authorities concluded that the explosive was too dangerous for use in battle! The Swedish military would not deal with the Nobels anymore. So Alfred looked for other applications for his explosive. He went to Paris, looking for a loan to finance their experiments. He approached the Société de Credit Mobilier that specialized in financing railroad construction and other public works. They listened with interest to Alfred's presentation and granted him a loan of 100,000 francs (F). With his financial worries solved, Alfred started researching how to produce a controlled explosion.

When the Nobels developed the explosive oil, it attracted considerable attention. Alfred and his father would, in 1868, share the Letterstedt Prize awarded by the Swedish Academy of Sciences for the invention and development of dynamite. Alfred, during his career, time and again, bridged the gap between theory and application. Kenne Fant called him "the inventor of the impossible" in his biography, *Alfred Nobel*. Scientists in the field of explosives have declared that his work on initial ignition is "the greatest progress in explosive-substance technique since the invention of black gunpowder." The age of nitroglycerin began when, in 1864, Alfred Nobel produced an explosion with pure nitroglycerin using a very small charge of gunpowder.

Alfred's most important invention was the detonating cap. The story behind this invention is a classic illustration of the way the mind of a scientist-inventor works. Let's fast-forward a few years in the future when Alfred was living in Paris at the Avenue Malakoff in the early 1870s. Alfred had a cut in his finger that kept him awake at night. He put on it some collodion (a highly flammable solution of pyroxylin, ether, and alcohol, used as an adhesive to close small wounds, among other applications). But the collodion flaked out and Alfred woke up in pain. He went back to his laboratory to apply more collodion to his wound. But then, at 4:00 a.m. in his laboratory, he started thinking about the chemical composition of collodion. It was created by dissolving cellulose nitrate in ether and alcohol. When the ether evaporated, a gelatinous mass remained. Alfred began adding drops of nitroglycerin to the mass. After numerous trials and errors, he succeeded in forming a blasting gelatin or rubber dynamite.

The Explosion

But now, let's go back to Heleneborg, Sweden, 1864. In the Nobel laboratory, the nitroglycerin research team consisted of Alfred, his father, an engineer, an errand boy, a servant girl, and Alfred's younger brother Emil. On Saturday, September 3, 1864, Emil and a friend named Hartzman were busy purifying glycerin. They were manufacturing the explosive for an order from the Ammberg and Northern Railways. Alfred had received his Swedish patent for nitroglycerin mixed with gunpowder. There were some 250 pounds of explosive oil stored in the shed. Suddenly, the shed exploded with a terrible roar. The following are excerpts from a newspaper account:

> There was nothing left of the factory, a wooden building adjacent to the Heleneborg estate, except a few charred fragments thrown here and there . . . Most ghastly was the sight of the mutilated corpses strewn on the ground. Not only had the clothes been torn off but on some the head was missing and the flesh ripped off the bones. These formless masses of flesh and bone bore little resemblance to a human body. . . . in a nearby stone house, the walls facing the factory had split open, and a woman who had been standing by the stove cooking had part of her head crushed, one arm torn off, and one thigh terribly mauled. The unfortunate was still alive and was carried to the hospital on a litter, looking more like a bloody mass than a human being.
>
> No trace has as yet been found of engineer Nobel's youngest son. (Although some thought that they recognized the youngest member of the Nobel family among the corpses).
>
> The youngest son of engineer Nobel, Emil Nobel, and the technology student Hartzman were involved in preparing some experiments to make the glycerine liquid more explosive, when some carelessness must

have triggered the explosion, which then spread to other nitroglycerine kept in open containers. Nitroglycerine is not combustible until heated up to 180 degrees Celsius or more, or through an explosion of some other substance on its surface.

The engineer Bloom and an older son of engineer Nobel, Alfred Nobel, were thrown to the floor by the violent pressure and severely injured in the face and head by fragments of wood and glass.

Alfred remained silent about the accident his whole life. On September 5, 1864, Immanuel wrote in the newspaper *Stockholm Dagblad* a detailed account of his analysis of the probable cause of the accident:

Because nitroglycerine is innocuous even when directly ignited—even the greatest carelessness with fire hardly would cause an explosion—and because there was no fire to begin with, there remains as the only possible explanation that the tests my son was doing brought about a reaction that increased the temperature of the mixture to a temperature (around 180 degrees Celsius) at which nitroglycerine explodes. In other words, the cause of the accident was negligence, in the form of not using a thermometer during a new experiment in order to read the temperature before it rose too rapidly.

The accident took a toll on Immanuel a month later. On October 6, he suffered a stroke that impaired his ability to move. He never fully recovered until his death eight years later.

Despite the accident, Alfred never gave up on nitroglycerin. He knew that there were practical applications that ensured a bright future for the explosive. The mines in Dannemora and Herräng ordered large quantities of nitroglycerin. Only five weeks after the explosion, the state railroads announced that they would use only Nobel's explosive oil in the construction of a tunnel that would connect the northern and southern railroads.

Alfred planned the creation of a company for the manufacture of nitroglycerin. After the explosion, the habitants of Stockholm did not approve of the Nobel's work and considered it unsafe. Obtaining capital to fund the company was not easy. But two important financial backers supported the Nobels. Captain Carl Wennëstrom of the navy mechanical corps and the King of Kungsholm, J. W. Smitt, who had made his fortune in South America and was one of Sweden's richest men. On October 24, 1864, Nitroglycerine Aktiebolaget was formed—the world's first nitroglycerin manufacturing company.

A major problem at the outset was the ailing Immanuel's demand to be the company's managing director. Alfred wanted the position for himself. Alfred's brother Robert, who had obtained a patent for nitroglycerin in Finland, served as mediator between Alfred and Immanuel. Robert wrote his brother Ludvig about his efforts to convince Immanuel to desist from being managing director and leave the post to Alfred. He wrote: "I do not really like Alfred's line of conduct either. He is too fierce and despotic and the two of them are heading for a collision." Eventually, a compromise was reached, and Carl Wennërstrom was elected managing director. Immanuel was offered a deputy position on the board of directors and eventually became a full director.

Another major problem for the new company was the prohibition by the police against the "manufacture and storing of nitroglycerin within a residential area." Alfred came up with a clever solution: he bought a covered barge and anchored it in Bockholm Bay and manufactured Nobel's patented explosive oil on board. So the industry that in a few years would extend around the world started on the water outside Stockholm. A year after the founding of the company, Carl Wennërstrom retired as managing director. His successor, J. A. Berndes, died after one month (during that month, he succeeded in embezzling 2,000 crowns [kr]), and Robert Nobel was elected managing director. Alfred was content with a deputy position since he was planning greater things. On January 21, 1865, Alfred got permission to build a factory on land at Winter Bay. This was the first land-based nitroglycerin factory.

Dynamite

In 1866, several catastrophic accidents occurred around the world involving nitroglycerin. A steamship exploded near Panama's Atlantic coast with 47 persons killed. Shortly afterward, the German ship *Mosel*, on its way to New York, was demolished before leaving Bremerhaven when a shipment of nitroglycerin detonated with 84 persons killed and 184 injured. In Australia, a large number of persons died when a warehouse exploded. Two crates with 350 pounds of nitroglycerin were stored in the building. And to make matters worse, Alfred's factory outside Hamburg exploded. Alfred had travelled to New York to establish a nitroglycerin factory in the United States. The press referred to him as the "travelling salesman of death" among other terrible things that hurt Alfred deeply.

In the United States, Alfred had to defend himself against the machinations of a man who called himself Colonel Shaffner and "the world's leading expert on military underwater mines." Colonel Shaffner wanted to obtain the patent for the United States but offered Alfred an insultingly low price for it: 10,000 Spanish dollars of little value. Colonel Shaffner challenged Alfred's American patent for the invention of nitroglycerin by claiming that he had made the discovery first (he had obtained information on the Nobel method to detonate nitroglycerin from the diplomatic representative in Stockholm). Alfred successfully defended his invention in an American court. But the US Congress passed the so-called anti-nitroglycerin law on July 26, 1866. Punishment for those responsible for an explosion was prison. Transport of blasting oil was permitted only if the crates were labeled Dangerous And nitroglycerin had to be stored in containers designed by Shaffner for which he had been granted a patent. So the colonel had his victory after all.

Alfred never returned to the United States. He explained to a colleague in a letter: "Life in America was not pleasant to me in the long run. The exaggerated stress over money destroys too many of the pleasures of society and ruins the sense of honor for the sake of imaginary needs."

Upon his return from America, Alfred was determined to find a safer way to package his nitroglycerin without reducing its explosive power. He went back to the research he had begun three years earlier. He used a material known as kieselguhr that consisted of hardened algae as fine as powder and was abundant along the banks of the Elbe and Alsten rivers. He mixed 75 percent nitroglycerin with 25 percent kieselguhr and produced a highly explosive solid. He called his invention dynamite from the Greek *dynamis*, which means "power" (and maybe from the name of an electric generator—dynamo). Dynamite was easy to handle, almost risk-free, with great explosive power. His Swedish patent was dated September 19, 1866. The full trade name of the new product was Dynamite or Nobel's Safety Powder. Soon, he was known across Germany as *Der Dynamiten-koning* (the dynamite king).

Nobel intended dynamite to be used for peaceful construction projects. But terrorists found it a convenient means for political murder. Czar Alexander II of Russia barely escaped an attempt against his life in February 1880 when a load of dynamite exploded beneath his dining room at the Winter Palace. Little over a year later, he was killed by a dynamite-filled bomb thrown against his carriage in the center of Saint Petersburg.

Alfred had factories and laboratories in some ninety different places in more than twenty countries. He traveled extensively between 1866 and 1872. Victor Hugo once described him as "Europe's richest vagabond." He had financial dealings in most European countries. In 1873, when his most hectic travel days came to an end, he settled in Paris. He felt that Paris was the center of business and cultural life. He bought a splendid house at 53 Avenue de Malakoff (by strange coincidence, when he and his father were helping the Russian military place mines in the Finnish Bay during the Crimean War, one of the most famous fortresses of the city of Sevastopol was called Malakov). Today, Avenue de Malakaoff, renamed Avenue Raymond Poincare, and the house renumbered 74, serves as the embassy of the Lao People's Democratic Republic.

With fame and fortune came hundreds of letters begging for monetary donations. Alfred wrote that each morning, the mail brought two dozen requests for money amounting to 20,000 kr (then about $4,000) or 7 million kr annually ($1.4 million), "which is why I must state that it would be better to have a reputation for being miserly than being generous." And generous he was—although he had to "separate wheat from chaff." But there is an anecdote that a woman employed in his household was getting married. When Alfred asked what she wanted as a wedding gift, she jokingly replied, "As much as Monsieur Nobel himself earns in a day." Amused, Alfred agreed, and we can only imagine the surprise of the young woman and her husband when they saw a bank draft from Alfred for the sum of ₣40,000 (today equivalent of $110,000)!

Ascanio Sobrero

Let's pay tribute to the discoverer of nitroglycerin, the Italian chemist Ascanio Sobrero. Sobrero was born on October 12, 1812, in Casale Monferrato. He studied medicine in Turin and Paris and then chemistry at the University of Giessen with Justus Liebeig and earned a doctorate in 1832. In 1845, he became a professor at the University of Turin. In 1846, Sobrero combined nitric acid with sulfuric acid and created oil with highly explosive qualities. He called it pyroglycerine. He warned vigorously against its use in letters and in a journal article. Sobrero badly scarred his face when a test tube with a small amount of nitroglycerin exploded. He felt that the substance was too dangerous to handle. He was so scared of it that he kept it secret for over a year. For a long time, nitroglycerin was considered a scientific curiosity because it was so dangerous. Sobrero wrote: "When I think of all the victims killed during nitroglycerine explosions, and the terrible havoc that has been wrecked, which in all probability will continue to occur in the future, I am almost ashamed to admit to be its discoverer."

When Alfred Nobel took nitroglycerin and successfully marketed it and later invented dynamite, Ascanio was mortified and felt that he had suffered an injustice by not receiving proper credit for being the inventor of nitroglycerin.

Alfred was always deferential to Sobrero. In a letter dated May 25, 1879, Alfred addresses Sobrero as "Highly Esteemed Professor!" and states "The whole world owes you a debt of gratitude for your significant invention. Your affectionate A. Nobel."

Alfred hired Sobrero as a consultant in his Swedish-Italian firm in Avigliana. In 1879, he erected a bust of Sobrero outside that plant. After Sobrero's death on May 26, 1888, at age seventy-five, Nobel awarded his widow a lifetime pension.

Sobrero may have been the discoverer of nitroglycerin, but it was Nobel who found practical (engineering) applications for it. He also marketed it. Kenne Fant wrote: "Not for the first time in history has an invention proven it needed two talents: that of the creator and that of the exploiter."

Bertha

In 1876, Alfred decided that he needed a highly qualified secretary to help him with his correspondence and record keeping. He placed an advertisement in a Viennese newspaper that read "Wealthy, highly educated elderly gentleman seeks lady of mature age, versed in languages, as secretary and supervisor of household." He called himself "elderly" although he was barely forty-three. The lady would need to write letters in five languages and be versed in history, literature, and preferably music. I don't know why he also wanted her to be able to cook.

He received many responses, but one caught his attention because the handwriting and the elegant choice of words indicated that the applicant was highly qualified. She was Countess Bertha Sofia Felitas Kinski von Chinic und Tettau (we will refer to her as Countess Bertha Kinski). She was thirty-three and unmarried. She came from one of the most aristocratic families in Austria.

Despite her aristocratic family, Bertha had a difficult childhood (her father was a poor military man in Vienna) and had to enter into service as governess for the daughters of the wealthy Baroness von Suttner. The family's young son, Arthur, fell in love with Bertha, who was seven years his senior. His mother opposed marriage between them in part because of the difference in age and also because of the meager dowry that Bertha would bring. The baroness read Alfred's ad in the newspaper and encouraged Bertha to apply for the position as a way to take her away from her son. Alfred eagerly replied to her letter, and after they agreed on her salary, she left for Paris.

When Alfred met Bertha at the train station in Paris, both were pleased at what they saw. She was pleasantly surprised that he was younger than the "elderly gentleman" that she expected. And Alfred found her as beautiful as he imagined. The house at Avenue de Malakoff was being remodeled, so Alfred reserved for her a suite at the Grand Hotel on the Boulevard des Capucines. She was pleased with the house at Avenue Malakoff, especially with the well-stocked library. When talking with Bertha, Alfred was at ease. He found in her an inspiring conversational partner. In his summary of Alfred Nobel's life and work, Kenne Fant wrote, "He falls in love with her almost immediately . . ."

According to Bertha's diary, Alfred told her, "I would like to invent a substance or machine so frightfully effective and devastating that it would forever make wars altogether impossible." These were Alfred's thoughts seventy-five years before the invention of the atomic bomb. Bertha wrote in her diary that "To speak with him about the world and people, about life and art, about problems of the moment or eternal problems, was an exquisite pleasure." It was clear to Bertha that Alfred needed someone to take care of him, someone who would be more than just a skilled secretary.

One or two days later, during a lunch in the Bois de Boulogne, Alfred asked Bertha if her heart was taken. Tactfully, Bertha explained that she was engaged to Arthur von Suttner, and she had responded to Alfred's ad because she needed to be financially independent.

After Bertha had been in Paris only a week, Alfred had to leave the country for urgent business. He was gone from May 9 to May 30, 1876. When he returned, he found that Bertha had paid the hotel bill (she sold a pin inherited from a relative and used the money to pay the hotel and buy a train ticket to Vienna). She returned to Vienna where she married Arthur von Suttner on June 12, 1876, without his parent's knowledge.

Alfred found himself alone and assumed that Bertha found him ridiculous. He thought he could never be able to get a "woman of the world" interested in him. A historian should remain objective when writing about a historical character. But there is a touch of a poet in me that feels great empathy for Alfred in his loneliness. How I wish I could have been his friend in his time and convince him that he was one of the most eligible bachelors of Europe. He could have married one of the most beautiful and highly educated women of his time. No historical account that I have read show that anybody, family or friend, tried to convince him of this. It appears that he lived the rest of his life in love with Bertha von Suttner Kinski. In his depression and sadness, Alfred met a beautiful and charming flower girl named Sophie Hess, then twenty-two, at the health resort Baden bei Wien, near Vienna. He started a relationship with her that lasted almost two decades. Kenne Fant devotes many pages of his excellent biography of Alfred Nobel to the letters exchanged between Alfred and Sophie. Eventually, she was unfaithful to Alfred, having a child with a young Austrian cavalry officer. Alfred ended his relationship with Sophie, but mercifully, he provided her with a modest pension. That is all I want to say about the affair with Sophie Hess. It is, I consider, a very sad episode in the life of a remarkable man.

It is more important to mention that Alfred and Bertha remained friends for the rest of his life, and they wrote and visited each other. Bertha von Suttner became a writer and published several novels. Eventually, she became critical of the arms race and wrote a famous book, *Lay Down Your Arms*, that made her a prominent figure in the peace movement. She definitely influenced Alfred who, in his will, included a Peace Prize. In 1905, Bertha won the Nobel Peace Prize.

Alfred's Industrial Empire

By 1873, Alfred ran twelve dynamite factories. He worked hard, managing his enterprises as a way to keep depression at bay. He learned the hard way that success in one part of his businesses was often followed by financial losses in other parts. Demand for dynamite sometimes did not meet expectations. And governments sometimes passed laws that hampered his businesses. In 1869, the British parliament passed the Nitroglycerine Act, which prohibited "manufacture, import, marketing, and transport of nitroglycerine and all substances of whatever kind that might contain the same within Great Britain." The person behind the law was Sir Frederick Abel, chief chemist of the war ministry, who—ten years earlier—had been granted a patent for the manufacturing process of guncotton (cotton powder). Dynamite was a potential competitor for him. When a colleague of Alfred, John Downie, requested a dispensation from the minister of the interior, he received a reply that stated that explosive substances could be permitted as long as they were manufactured at the site where they were to be used. It was the transport that was deemed too risky. It took lengthy negotiations with Sir Vivian Majendie, inspector of explosives, that Alfred got permission to start production of dynamite in Britain but had to comply with a long list of rigorous safety rules. The result was the British Dynamite Co. Ltd., founded in 1870. The plant was built at Ardeer, on Scotland's western coast. The plant was a model industrial complex that consisted of forty-five buildings, employed hundreds of workers and manufactured 5.5 million pounds of explosives per year. The press's sensationalistic coverage of accidents involving nitroglycerin and dynamite resulted in the absolute prohibition of transporting nitroglycerine products on English railroads. The law remained on the books for two decades.

In 1875, Alfred invented blasting gelatin in order to reduce the risk of accidents. But it took him until 1881 to obtain permission to manufacture it in the Ardeer factory.

Ludvig and Robert

Of the three Nobel brothers, Alfred and Ludvig were the most successful. Ludvig had the gift of dealing with people and machines. He made others feel good, an ability that served him well through his career. His machine shop in Saint Petersburg successfully built and sold mines, guns, and cannons for the military, as well as steam hammers and hydraulic presses for the civilian market.

All his life, Robert, the oldest brother and the least successful businessman, felt inferior to his brothers. One of Robert's businesses was a store that sold lamps and lamp oil. Robert joked that it was "a brilliant business in every way except financially." Alfred offered Robert the opportunity to market nitroglycerin in Finland. As soon as Robert established a nitroglycerin factory outside Helsinki, the czar announced his intention to prohibit manufacture of explosives in the Grand Duchy of Finland. Robert had to close shop.

When the managing director's position at Winter Bay became vacant, Alfred offered it to Robert. For little over three years, Robert ran the company. But it quickly became obvious that Robert did not have the ability that Ludvig had to work with people. He got himself on a collision course with important people such as multimillionaire and cofinancer Johan Wilhem Smitt and engineer Alarick Liedbeck, a longtime friend of Alfred and his most influential adviser. In 1870, Ludvig made Robert a partner in Ludvig's extremely successful mechanical business in Saint Petersburg. While Ludvig was in a seven-month honeymoon with his second wife (his first wife had died a year earlier), Robert signed an agreement with Peter Bildurling, the head of a gun factory in Issjevsk near the Ural Mountains, to manufacture Berdanka rifles for the Russian Army. Ludvig sent Robert on an assignment to visit other gun factories in Europe and buy a large quantity of first-class walnut wood for rifle butts at Baku in the Caucasus. At Baku, Robert became infected with naphtha fever. The skipper of the boat that took him to Baku owned a small refinery and several oil wells. Robert was familiar with the oil business since he imported Russian paraffin oil for his Helsinki lamp business. He obtained some capital from Ludvig and purchased the boat captain's oil wells and refinery. Ludvig wrote to Alfred, proposing that they travel to Baku to help Robert establish his oil business. Ludvig and his son Emanuel made the trip in 1876 (Alfred would not be talked into making the trip). Together, Robert and Ludvig acted on a seven-mile-long pipeline to transport oil from the oil wells to the refinery. Robert improved the refining process to obtain a first-rate light kerosene (the American name for naphtha). The Nobel era—in the Russian oil industry had begun.

Robert was a pioneer of environmental engineering by introducing smokeless combustion in a new refinery he built near his wells. This technology avoided adding pollution into the air of the region. By using special coolers for the waste, he was able to do ten distillations per day while his competitors were able to do only one distillation per day. The high quality of his kerosene made him the only one in the region capable of competing with American oil. Eventually, American oil companies stopped exporting oil to Russia as Robert and Ludvig expanded production.

In 1879, the Naphtha Production Stock-Company Brothers Nobel was founded, known as Branobel. But Robert ran the company for only a few years. Given his inability to work with people, he refused to work with a board of directors and retired at the age to fifty-two. Ludvig then became the uncrowned king of Russian oil. He was a brilliant entrepreneur without peer in Russia. Branobel became one of the largest oil companies in the world by the late nineteenth century, handling 30 percent of Russian exports of kerosene and 50 percent of the sales of lubricating oil to other countries. About 12 percent of the money left to establish the Nobel Prizes came from Alfred's shares in the company. During the Russian revolution, on April 28, 1920, the Bolsheviks took power in Baku and nationalized Branobel's oil business. Emanuel's son, Gösta Nobel, did a profitable masterstroke for the Nobel family: he sold almost half of Branobel's shares to Standard Oil of New Jersey. It was thought at the time that the Bolshevik regime would not last. Branobel was formally dissolved in 1959; its last president was Nils-Oleinikoff, a grandson of Ludvig Nobel.

Ludvig

By the early 1880s, Ludvig Nobel had become the uncrowned king of Russian oil. He was a brilliant entrepreneur. In addition to building an oil pipeline, he conceived the idea of building the world's first oil tanker. When Russian shipbuilders showed no interest in his idea, he contacted Swedish shipbuilder and chief engineer Sven Almquist who immediately got to work to build the *Zoroaster*, which sailed into Baku in March 1878 with 250 tons of oil. Swedish shipyards received orders from Ludvig for fifty-three oil tankers (or oil cistern steamers, as they were called) for a total of ten million Swedish crowns. Ludvig proudly boasted that he provided Swedish shipyards with six years of business. Ludvig had an incredible energy and capacity for work. At one time, he was responsible for oil production in Baku, Nobel's machine factory in Saint Petersburg, the rifle factory in Issyevsk, and the Nobel Brothers Company's board of directors in Saint Petersburg. His new distillation method in Baku extracted 35 percent of kerosene from oil while competitors barely extracted 20 percent. The Nobels owned forty oil wells on the oil fields of Balakhani. The pipeline system had the capacity to transport four million barrels per year. The company owned a fleet of twenty oil tankers on the Caspian Sea, twelve on the river Volga, and one thousand five hundred rail cars for railroad freight.

The Nobel industries employed between five thousand and ten thousand persons. Ludvig took great pride in providing his employees with as good a work environment as possible, including guaranteed salaries well above average, and ensured that his employees were paid on time (not typical in Russia). Ludvig built housing for his employees and financed the establishment of schools and libraries, hospitals, and recreational facilities. He was the first employer to include his personnel in discussions of profit sharing—over the loud protests of the Russian industrialists. Ludvig acquired a national reputation as an exemplary employer. His employees considered themselves "nobelites." Alfred shared his brother's sense of responsibility toward his employees; it was a family tradition.

Ludvig eventually had financial troubles because, as Alfred wrote to him, "A serious problem is that you build first and then look around for the necessary money." In 1883, Alfred had to visit Ludvig at Saint Petersburg to help him solve financial difficulties, but that is another story. Kenne Fant wrote several chapters in his book about Ludvig's troubles. But my purpose for writing this short narrative about Ludvig was to explain the importance of his death. When Ludvig died of a heart attack on April 12, 1888, at the age of fifty-seven, a French newspaperman thought it was Alfred who had died. Because Alfred had also been involved in the weapons industry (Alfred had invented new gunpowder for cannons), the obituary referred to Alfred as a "merchant of death" who had built a fortune by discovering new ways to "mutilate and kill." Alfred read this in his laboratory in Sevran. He was terribly pained, and he never forgot it. He became obsessed with his posthumous reputation and rewrote his last will, leaving most of his fortune to create what are today called the Nobel Prizes. So the genesis of the Nobel Prizes was an unfortunate case of mistaken identity. In

1893, Alfred bought the Swedish armaments works at Bofors. It is an apparent contradiction that he thought that manufacturing cannons for armies would bring peace. He was quoted, saying, "May factories make an end of war sooner than your congresses. The day when two army corps can annihilate each other in one second, all civilized nations, it is to be hoped, will recoil from war and discharge their troops." This was a curious anticipation of the Cold War, between 1946 and 1992, where the United States and its allies in the North Atlantic Treaty Organization faced the Soviet Union and the Warsaw Pact nations using nuclear deterrence to prevent World War III. And I was part of the nuclear deterrence as an intercontinental ballistic missile officer. But that is another story.

In 1887, Alfred said to Bertha von Suttner and her husband when they visited Paris, "I should like to be able to create a substance or a machine with such horrific capacity for mass annihilation that wars would become impossible forever."

In 1890, Bertha published her book, *Lay Down Arms*, which was met with worldwide success, and she sent Alfred a copy of its Swedish translation. Alfred wrote to her a letter referring to her book as a masterpiece and said, "It ought to be read and reflected upon by each and every one." But in their exchange of letters, it appears that Alfred was not convinced that Bertha's peace strategy was the best. In 1892, he wrote a letter to her that said,

> I do not believe that it is foremost the money that is lacking, but a real program. Good intentions alone will not assure peace, nor one might say, will great banquets and long speeches. You must have an acceptable plan to lay before the governments. To demand disarmament is ridiculous and will gain nothing.

In a letter written by Alfred in November 1892 to a retired Turkish diplomat, Aristarchi Bey, he wrote, "A declaration should be made that any and every aggressor would have all of Europe against him." These were prophetic of the role of the North Atlantic Treaty Organization (NATO). Alfred believed that, through formal treaties, governments would be duty-bound to defend collectively any attacked country, and afterward, partial disarmament would take place. But he would not recommend dismantling of all armies "since there has to be an armed force to maintain order."

Ballistite

In the late 1870s, the war ministries of nearly every European country were demanding improved military explosives. Dynamite could not be loaded into cannons, so Alfred spent years researching how to develop better gunpowder. The process is called phlegmatizing—that is, to produce a slower combustion of the gunpowder. He kept detailed journals of his research and experiments over an eight-year period. For a long time, the efforts of Alfred and his assistant, Georges Fehrenbach, were leading nowhere. In 1884, they finally succeeded in transforming high-explosive blasting substances into a stronger smokeless gunpowder. For various reasons, Alfred waited three years before seeking a French patent. He created gunpowder that produced only steam when it burned and was therefore smokeless. He called it ballistite. In Sweden, it was called Nobel-powder and explosives specialists called it C-89. The slow-burning ballistite was a combination of nitroglycerine, nitrocellulose, and camphor. Ballistite was a revolutionary invention for the munitions industry, especially in its applications to artillery pieces and shells. Ballistite was considered by many as Alfred's most disturbing invention. Alfred hoped that its deterrent aspect would prevent future wars.

Since Alfred had used the French firing ranges for his experiments, he offered his invention to the French government. However, the French declined because they felt they already had the same product. Chemistry professor P. M. E. Vielle had produced an almost smokeless gunpowder that he had named Sarrau-Vieille, Poudre B. He had contacts among influential politicians, and the powder was already being used by the French military.

In 1889, Alfred signed a contract with the Italian government for the delivery of three hundred tons of ballistite. A factory at Avigliana would manufacture it. But then the French gunpowder monopoly, the Administration des Poudres et Salpêtres, asserted that Alfred had inappropriately exploited the principle extended to him by the French government to let him use their shooting ranges. The patriotic press accused Alfred of espionage and treason. Alfred was banned from the shooting ranges and forbidden to manufacture ballistite at his dynamite factory in Honfleur. His laboratory was searched by the police, and the sample stock was confiscated.

Alfred took it very hard to have doubts cast upon his integrity and honor. French authorities let him know that he was persona non grata. This was immediately exploited by his competitors. Paul Barbe, Alfred's corporate partner in France who had served as France's minister of agriculture, tried to use his connections to help Alfred but to no avail. None of the well-informed persons who knew Alfred's great services to France would come to his defense. Learning that the campaign against him had been sanctioned at the highest levels and the police breaking into his laboratory convinced Alfred to leave France. In 1890, he left for San Remo, Italy. He purchased an Italian villa originally named Mio Nido—My Nest. Alfred changed its name to Villa Nobel after a friend mentioned that "a nest should have two birds." Alfred installed his laboratory in San Remo.

The climate in Italy was better for his health. Alfred suffered poor health most of his life, especially in his later years. In San Remo, Alfred and Robert exchanged letters about sickness and death. Alfred wrote to Robert that he did not want to be buried; he was terrified of being buried alive. He wrote instructions that his body be "dipped in hot sulfuric acid. That way the whole thing is done in one minute."

Alfred constantly suffered indigestion and headaches and possibly symptoms of chronic depression. In 1890, he complained of intense pain from angina pectoris (caused by inadequate flow of blood and oxygen to the heart). His physician prescribed nitroglycerin! Today, medical science knows that nitroglycerin is a prodrug; inactive by itself, it becomes active in the body (in vivo) by releasing nitric oxide. Nitric oxide then travels to the ischemic tissues of the cardiac arteries and dilates smooth muscle. In 1896, seven weeks before his death, Alfred wrote to a friend, "Isn't it the irony of fate that I have been prescribed nitroglycerin to be taken internally! They call it trinitrin, so as not to scare the chemist and the public."

The Cordite Affair

In 1890, while Alfred was being attacked by the press in France over the sale of ballistite to Italy and French police raided Alfred's laboratory, the managers of the Ardeer factory sent more bad news. Frederic Abel and physics professor James Dewar had received a patent for smokeless gunpowder that was almost identical to ballistite. Alfred was stunned that two men who, for years, had been his consultants and had been paid generous fees and considered friends by Alfred could be capable of stealing his invention. Alfred informed the management of Nobel's Explosives that he wanted to settle out of court. Normally, Alfred's word was law, but Alfred did not have a majority interest in the company. Against Alfred's wishes, the management and lawyers of Nobel's Explosives filed a lawsuit that turned out to be lengthy, strenuous, and expensive.

In 1888, the English government had appointed an explosives committee to investigate new inventions that could have an effect on military explosive substances and advise the war department about which technical developments to adopt. Frederic Abel and James Dewar were the committee's most prominent members. Abel and Dewar applied for and received information about ballistite. The commission recommended that camphor be exchanged for acetone. Abel and Dewar meanwhile experimented in their own state laboratory and produced a nearly smokeless powder that consisted of 58 percent nitroglycerine, 37 percent cotton powder, and 5 percent Vaseline (gelatinized with acetone at Alfred's suggestion). The substance was named cordite because it was pressed into strings or cords. Abel and Dewar kept their patent secret for years in order to get more information out of Alfred.

When Nobel's Explosives offered ballistite to the war ministry, Abel and Dewar's patent came to light. Then Nobel's Explosives learned that Abel and Dewar had surrendered their patent to the English government but kept the foreign rights. They recommended to the war ministry that their cordite be adopted instead of ballistite. In court, Abel and Dewar admitted to have had knowledge of Alfred's experiments but insisted that in no way had that privilege influenced the creation of cordite. They stated that there were differences between the patent descriptions of cordite and ballistite. To Alfred, the differences were meaningless. This was a question of honor.

For three long years, the case was in court: first in the chancery division, then at the Courts of Appeals, and finally at the House of Lords. The court based its judgment on a vague reference in Alfred's patent description where he referred to "the ingredient nitrocellulose of the well-known soluble kind." The court ruled that this eliminated everything that was "insoluble." In vain, Alfred's attorneys proved to the court that insoluble nitrocellulose powder, under certain conditions, could be soluble. In 1895, the court rejected the Nobel's Explosives claim for damage for patent encroachment, and it had to pay £28,000 in court costs.

One of the three judges during the final pleading gave Alfred moral support. The judge explained that for strictly judicial reasons, he had to join his two cojudges in rejecting the Nobel's Explosives demand. But he said, "Mr. Nobel has made a significant invention which is theoretical remarkable and truly new—and then two skillful chemists get hold of the patent description, study it carefully, and discover that by using practically the same ingredients and with only minor modification they could achieve the same result. It must be considered urgent to see to it that, if possible, this does not occur in a way that deprives Mr. Nobel of the value of an exceptionally significant patent."

But Alfred was robbed of his invention. Alfred's view of the courts and lawyers in particular was more bitter and fierce than before. He referred to lawyers as "blood-suckers who devour fortunes after delivering short-sighted interpretations of meaningless court rulings, whose obscurity darkens even darkness itself."

Alfred wrote a satirical play called *The Patent Bacillus* based on the cordite affair. Regretfully, only a few scattered pages remain that are incomprehensible to anyone not familiar with the cordite case.

Ragnar Sohlman

In 1893, Alfred met a twenty-three-year-old engineer named Ragnar Sohlman, who became an extraordinarily loyal associate and a close friend. Alfred's mother and his brother Ludvig had passed away, and his affair with Sophie Hess had ended. Alfred was lonely and needed a friend.

After graduating from the Technical Institute at Stockholm, Ragnar worked in a dynamite factory in the United States owned by the DuPonts. In 1893, he was offered a job as engineer at an explosive-substance factory in Mexico, but illness kept him from accepting it. During the summer of 1893, while working in the Swedish pavilion at the Chicago World's fair, he was surprised to receive a telegram offering him the job as Alfred Nobel's personal assistant. It was thirty-seven years later (on his own sixtieth birthday) that Ragnar found out who recommended him for the job: Alfred's chief financial backer in Winter Bay, J. W. Smitt, and Robert's son, Ludvig.

In October 1893, "with certain trepidation," Ragnar Sohlman met Alfred at a hotel in Paris. Ragnar's first project was to organize Alfred's library at Avenue de Malakoff. He grouped the technical and scientific books by subject and the literary works by language. Alfred was very pleased with the result. But Alfred quickly realized that Ragnar did not possess the language skills that his secretary needed. So Alfred employed Ragnar at his laboratory in San Remo where he became one of his favorite people. Ragnar became a valued addition to the laboratory at San Remo. Among his duties was maintaining Alfred's extensive patent correspondence. Ragnar had great respect for his employer and insisted on calling him Doctor even after he had been asked not to. Alfred said in 1895, "if somebody as thoroughly sound as Mr. Sohlman is willing to lend me a little friendship, I will indeed accept it and be glad for it."

Bofors Cannons

In October 1893, Alfred started planning the purchase of the Bofors machine works in Sweden. He wanted to turn it into a cannon industry with international scope "to see Sweden rival Germany and England when it comes to arms." He was looking forward to conduct his increasingly advanced weapon-technical experiments in a newly equipped laboratory. He planned to move his laboratory from San Remo to Bofors.

In January 1894, Alfred purchased Bofors for one million Swedish crowns. The industrial plant was antiquated and badly neglected. Alfred was well aware that he had acquired an enterprise on the brink of bankruptcy. In the first meeting of the board of directors of his new company, he was elected chairman of the board. Alfred quickly invested 2.5 million Swedish crowns for reconstruction. He built a new laboratory, the worn-out tool shops were refurbished, and the machine park for the manufacture of what would be the famous Bofors cannons was reconstructed.

Alfred demanded high quality not only in materials but in workers' performance. He "practiced honesty but not sentimentality." If a person in a position of responsibility did not measure up to his standards, Alfred could quickly fire him, regardless of his rank. But Alfred's concern for the well-being of his workers became famous. His philosophy was when people have been assured material security, only then can they be expected to contribute satisfactory work.

In August 1894, Ragnar Sohlman assumed the position of superintendent. Bofors became one of the most important cannon manufacturers in the world. Bofors cannons were manufactured by the Chrysler Corporation to be used by US Navy ships during World War II. The Bofors 40-mm gun is an anti-aircraft auto cannon. It was one of the most popular medium-weight anti-aircraft systems during World War II, used by most of the western Allies as well as by the Axis forces. It was used in many wars, including the Indo-Pakistani wars and conflicts, the Arab-Israeli conflicts, Korean War, Vietnam War, Falklands War, Gulf War, Yugoslav wars, Iraq War, and the Lebanese Civil War among others. The cannon remains in service as of 2013, making it one of the longest-serving artillery pieces of all time. It is often referred to simply as the Bofors gun. Today (2013), Bofors is still an important weapons producer in the world.

Alfred's Death

On the fall of 1896, Alfred had been told by his physician in Paris that his health was not good. Yet Alfred returned to San Remo. On December 7, 1896, Alfred suffered a stroke. He was carried to his bedroom by his servants. His manservant, Auguste Oswald, telegraphed Alfred's nephews and Sohlman immediately. Alfred Nobel died three days later on the morning of December 10. Neither Sohlman, Hjalmar, or Emanuel were able to reach San Remo in time. Alfred died alone, surrounded by paid servants.

Upon arriving to Villa Nobel, Salhman, Hjalmar, and Emanuel began a systematic search for valuable documents and money. They found the second last will that Alfred had annotated "Cancelled and replaced by a last will of December 27, 1895." They learned that this will was on file at Stockholm's Enskilda Bank. Solhman sent a telegram to the managing director of AB Bofors for a copy as soon as possible. On December 15, 1896, Emanuel received a telegram from the bank, informing that the will had been opened. Alfred had selected Solhman and Rudolph Liljequist to act as executors of his will and testament. It also asked that Alfred's arteries be opened and the corpse cremated.

After Solhman recovered from his surprise at having been chosen as executor, he contacted the physician who had signed the death certificate. The doctor was amazed at such request and explained that the actions that had been taken as part of the embalming process was as effective as cutting the arteries. Sohlman and Liljequist realized that Alfred Nobel's assets were located in several countries. They decided to move most of these assets to Sweden. To prevent French authorities from making claims to the money and blocking its transfer, the two engineers went round the banks in Paris with horse and carriage and collected the shares, bonds, and other documents belonging to the Nobel estate. They packed the documents into crates and shipped them to Sweden from a railroad station in Paris as registered luggage.

After funeral services were held and Alfred Nobel's body was cremated, the will was read and everyone was shocked. Alfred's last will left approximately 94 percent to the establishment of five prizes (physics, chemistry, physiology or medicine, literature, and peace) to "those who, during the preceding year, shall have conferred the greatest benefit on mankind."

But Alfred's relatives wanted the will contested. There were other problems with the will. The way it was written, it could have been contested in France.

The will stated that the literature prize was to be awarded to "whomever, within literature, has produced the most outstanding work in an 'ideal direction.'" The left-wing press criticized Alfred's decision to have the Swedish Academy award the prize since the academy was a very conservative institution and would be biased in its interpretation of the "ideal direction." It will never be possible to define what Alfred Nobel intended by the word *ideal*. It could be that Alfred meant "idealistic" instead of "ideal" since the two words are spelled very similarly in Swedish.

It is unclear why Alfred wanted the peace prize to be awarded in Norway, which—at the time of Alfred's death—was ruled in union with Sweden. Many considered Alfred to be unpatriotic for this decision. The Norwegian Nobel Committee speculates that Alfred chose Norway because it did not have the militaristic traditions of Sweden. Also, the Norwegian parliament was involved in the Inter-Parliamentary Union's efforts to resolve conflicts through mediation and arbitration.

The prizes in chemistry and physics were to be awarded by the Academy of Science while the prize for physiology or medicine would be awarded by the Karolinska Institute.

Other hurdles to implement the prizes included the following:

- The "fund" to implement the prizes did not exist and had to be created.
- The organizations that Nobel named in his will to award the prizes had not been asked to take on these duties prior to his death. There was no plan to compensate these organizations for their work on the prizes.
- The will gave no guidance on what to do if no prize winners for a year were found.

In February 1898, King Oscar II summoned Alfred's nephew, Emanuel, who was a Russian citizen. Oscar II felt that the fact that the prizes did not exclusively reward Swedish citizens was "unpatriotic." He told Emanuel that it was his duty to his sisters and brothers "to see to it that their interests are not neglected in favor of the fantastic ideas your uncle had." The king hinted that Alfred had been under the influence of "females"—referring to

Bertha von Suttner. Emanuel courageously replied, "Your Majesty! I will not expose my siblings to the risk that in the future they will be accused by highly deserving scientists of having appropriated for themselves what would rightly go toward science."

It took five years of hard work before the Nobel Foundation could be established and the first prizes awarded on the fifth anniversary of Alfred Nobel's death on December 10, 1901. Ragnar Sohlman was instrumental in establishing the Nobel Foundation and organizing its cooperation with the prize-awarding institutions. Ragnar worked for AB Bofors Nobelkrut from 1899 to 1919, becoming its chief executive officer. During 1929 to 1946, Ragnar Sohlman served as the executive director of the Nobel Foundation. He died in 1948.

Every year on December 10, the Nobel prizes are awarded in Stockholm and Oslo. The prizes are awarded independent of ideology, race, sex, or nationality.

In 1968, the Sveringes Riksbank, Sweden's central bank, established and endowed the Nobel Memorial Prize in Economic Sciences on the bank's 300th anniversary. The prize is awarded by the Royal Swedish Academy of Sciences for outstanding contributions in economic sciences. The first prize was awarded in 1969. It is the only non-Nobel prize that has ever been associated officially with the Nobel Foundation.

Kenne Fant's last words in his biography of Alfred Nobel were "[The Nobel prizes] have become an enduring monument to a brilliant inventor, a visionary empire builder, and an unprejudiced humanist."

John von Neumann
Mathematical Genius

How many of you have heard of John von Neumann? I learned about him by watching an old video when I was in college. We hear a lot about Albert Einstein and Robert Oppenheimer (the father of the atomic bomb) but seldom hear about von Neumann who was a contemporary of them. Von Neumann was instrumental in the development of the atomic bomb, the modern computer, game theory, and many other things. Economist Norman Macrae, who retired as the principal editor of *The Economist*, published in 1992 a wonderful biography about "Johnny," which was my principal source for this chapter.

Different from another famous mathematician, John Nash (*A Beautiful Mind*), Johnny was neither "odd" nor arrogant. He was described by Macrae as a "cherub," extremely polite and "an exceptionally well balanced man." In an old video, I saw him blowing into a tube that lighted a light bulb tied on top of his head. The video said that he loved these types of gadgets.

He was born Neumann Janos on December 28, 1903, in Budapest, Hungary, the son of a banker and, therefore, into an upper–middle class family. He quickly showed qualities of a genius. At the end of his secondary education, Johnny wanted to be a mathematician, but his practical father decided that he should be a chemical engineer (as a chemical engineer myself, I feel proud and flattered). Most the scientific geniuses born in

Hungary, contemporaries of Johnny, studied chemical engineering. But Johnny enrolled in the University of Zurich to study chemical engineering *and* in the University of Budapest to study a PhD in mathematics *simultaneously*. He graduated from his PhD in mathematics with the highest honors in 1926 and his undergraduate in chemical engineering when he was not yet twenty-three. But he was to work all his life as a mathematician and never as a chemical engineer (oh well, I always worked in related fields but never as a chemical engineer as such). As Norman Macrae wrote, Johnny "became the most quietly effective mathematical mind of this century." When analyzing a complex mathematical problem, Johnny would mutter to himself while staring at the ceiling (or at women's legs) and, within five minutes, would have a precise solution to the problem. He did not invent the computer or meteorological science or game theory, but he would "instantly leap an average of five blocks ahead of most people who brought a suggestion to him in making developments in these fields." While other mathematicians' presentation could be very boring, Johnny's were different in that he "did not work boringly in preparation. He just pandered on a train." He would write equations on a blackboard at what appeared to be the speed of light. During the period of 1927 to 1929, still in his twenties, Johnny was publishing one major mathematical paper per month—something extraordinary. This prodigious productivity made him world-famous and, eventually in 1930, got him an appointment as a lecturer at Princeton University in New Jersey. Later, Johnny became one of the first highly paid mathematicians of the Institute of Advanced Studies at Princeton.

Despite his incredible mathematical mind, Johnny was embarrassed by not remembering the faces or names of people who knew him (I have the same problem; I'm proud of having something else in common with Johnny, sort of).

His relations with women remained clumsy all his life. Women who knew him well liked him (and he liked children). But women who had just met him found him a bit odd. His wives found that he might ignore them if he was focused in his mathematical thinking. And he did not do any household work at home. His first wife, high society Hungarian Mariette Kovesi, six years his junior, was a vivacious and beautiful woman who loved to enjoy life. She definitely enjoyed life in the United States when Johnny moved to Princeton but eventually divorced Johnny and married one of his graduate students, Horner Kuper, and lived happily ever after.

Now let's talk a little about how John von Neumann got a driver's license in America. Johnny was the type of absent-minded scientist who could not pass a driving test under normal circumstances. But Mariette heard about a certain driving test instructor under the Brooklyn Bridge. You could pass the test by paying him ten dollars (a lot of money in the Depression era). So ladies and gentlemen, that is how Johnny was let loose on the roads of America. He liked to drive fast and on the center of the road. Then his mind would wander off to the complex analysis of some mathematical problem or another, and he would invariably end up crashing his car against a tree. How he did not get killed or seriously injured is a mystery. In one of those accidents, in Europe in 1934, Johnny and Mariette Kovesi had travelled to Genoa from New York to avoid travelling through Nazi Germany. Johnny's plan was to rent a car at Genoa to drive to Budapest. But his in-laws, the Kovesis, aware of Johnny's reputation as a driver, had their private car waiting for them at Genoa, including a trusted driver. But Johnny insisted on driving himself, fast, through Northern Italy and Austria and across the Hungarian border into wooded country in driving rain. When his mind wandered into the complexities of mathematics, he totaled the car against a tree. Mariette was thrown against the windshield and broke her nose in several places, requiring a lot of surgery. For many years, she insisted that this accident ruined her good looks. Eventually, after a series of spectacular accidents, Johnny finally figured out that it was safer and more productive to ride the train where he could work on his problems undisturbed. Sometimes, he would purchase a train ticket to a place far from home and a return ticket immediately after reaching its destiny so he could spend several hours working to his brain's satisfaction.

Von Neumann and the Atomic Bomb

Between 1937 and 1943, Johnny was a consultant on ballistics to the Ballistics Research Laboratory (BRL) of the US Army Ordnance Department at Aberdeen Proving Ground. In 1940, he was elevated to member of the BRL Scientific Advisory Board. He was also a consultant to the Ordnance Department of the US Navy. Johnny became a master calculator of complicated explosions, such as colliding ones. One of Johnny's discoveries during his involvement with the BRL was the principle that "large bombs are better detonated at a considerable altitude than on the ground." This principle was put to use with atomic bomb explosions at Hiroshima and Nagasaki. In 1987, I was certified by the US Army Chemical School as a "nuclear target analyst." I can also add that exploding nuclear weapons at high altitude also, as a bonus effect, prevent the production of radioactive fallout since the fireball would not touch the ground, picking up tons of dirt that would become radioactive and be spread over large areas by winds aloft.

After the attack on Pearl Harbor, the US Army first asked the Institute of Advanced Studies at Princeton for Albert Einstein's assistance with theoretical calculations for the Manhattan Project for the development of the atomic bomb. But soon after, a decision was made not to involve Einstein in the A-bomb project because of his past attitude as a pacifist. The intelligence community was concerned that he would be a security risk. Then in 1943, Johnny was recruited as a consultant for Los Alamos.

Johnny's two main contributions to the atomic bomb were the mathematicization of Los Alamos and the development of the implosion bomb. In the first contribution, Johnny was part of a team who invented modern mathematical modeling. To put it in simple terms, it was not possible to conduct experiments about how to blow up the world. So Johnny developed mathematical formulas that explained what would happen during such an explosion. Johnny excelled in making rough *order of magnitude* estimates mentally. An example of order of magnitudes is an estimate of size or magnitude expressed as a power of ten: Earth's mass is of the order of magnitude of 10^{22} tons; that of the sun is 10^{27} tons. Calculations at Los Alamos required a lot of order of magnitude estimates—at top level to introduce new concepts and at lower levels to save unnecessary calculations and keep the project on schedule. At the top, Hans Bethe, head of the theoretical division, said that Johnny taught him a lot of mathematics; there were differential equations that he could not solve, but Johnny would explain them to him with ease. At the bottom, whenever Johnny came out of a room, he would be besieged by groups of persons with questions about mathematical problems. Johnny would walk down the corridor, and by the time he got to the room for his next meeting, he would either have the answers or suggested shortcuts to get them. Calculations at Los Alamos in those days were being made by IBM punch-card sorters. Johnny was so impressed by them that he immediately started thinking on how to make them better. We will learn about his adventures with computers later.

But the really critical contribution of Johnny was to shorten the war by developing the lens for the implosion of plutonium (the Fat Man atomic bomb dropped on Nagasaki). To sustain a nuclear reaction that could result in an explosion, the nuclear material had to have supercritical mass. In the development of the atomic bomb, there were two types of fissile materials: uranium 235 and plutonium 239. The bomb dropped over Hiroshima used U-235. Its design was relatively simple, referred to as the gun method. A mass of U-235 is fired by a gun-like device into a cavity against another piece of U-235, and the two together achieve supercritical mass and explode. The problem was that U-235 occurs in nature as a very small portion of uranium; most of uranium is U-238. U-235 had to be separated from U-238 atom by atom in a very slow chemical process. However, the U-238 could be converted to plutonium-239 much faster by bombardment with neutrons. But shooting one piece of Pu-239 against another by the gun method did not work. So the scientists determined that to obtain supercritical mass of Pu-239, they would need to use an "implosion" method—that is, to surround a sphere of Pu-239 with a fat mass of high explosives (therefore the name Fat Man bomb) and detonate the explosives at the same time all around the Pu-239 so it could be "squeezed" into supercritical mass. But all attempts to conduct the implosion failed to create a supercritical mass of Pu-239. An English scientist, James Tuck, suggested the idea of implosion lens. The concept was that the outer layer of high explosives around the plutonium core should be fast burning. The inner layer—toward the thinner end of the lens pointing inward—would be slower burning. The idea was to allow the rest of the shock wave to catch up. Before hitting the plutonium, the shock wave would again be speeded up. The analogy was with an optical lens that directs light toward a focal point.

Physicist Hans Bethe, chief of the Theoretical Division at Los Alamos, and Johnny liked Tuck's idea and worked to device such a lens. According to Bethe, Johnny "very quickly devised an arrangement which was obviously correct from the theoretical point of view." Eventually, Robert Oppenheimer, director of Los Alamos, put chemist Kistiakowsky in June 1944 in charge of developing these lenses, and he spent several months turning this theory into practice. After a number of failures, the first satisfactory lens worked in December 1944. In March 1945, Oppenheimer ordered that a test explosion of Fat Man had to be done in New Mexico to be sure that it would work as a weapon against Japan. There was no doubt that the uranium bomb, Little Boy, would work, and it would be dropped on Hiroshima. But nobody was sure that these weird lenses would work—that is, nobody except a physicist called Klaus Fuchs who was spying for the Soviets. Fuchs passed details of Johnny's ideas to the Russians as fast as he could. The Trinity test on July 16, 1945, in New Mexico proved that Fat Man would work. The Trinity test achieved the equivalent of about twenty thousand tons of TNT.

Johnny became the principal Los Alamos calculator of the height from which to drop the bombs. At Aberdeen Proving Ground, Johnny had become the master calculator of complicated explosions. One of Johnny's discoveries during his involvement with the Ballistics Research Laboratory (BRL) was the principle that "large bombs are better detonated at a considerable altitude than on the ground." The idea was that the blast would affect the largest area possible instead of most of the explosion be directed upwards if the explosion happened on land. One of Johnny's findings was that if the detonation was 14 percent too high, the damage would be reduced by 24 percent. It was better to go too low rather than too high. This principle was put to good use with the atomic bomb explosions at Hiroshima and Nagasaki. Johnny made the calculations that determined at what altitude the A-bombs would explode over their targets. The final list of targets included three sites: Hiroshima, Kokura Arsenal, and Nagasaki. Colonel Paul Tibbets and the crew of Enola Gay hit Hiroshima on August 6, 1945, with Little Boy whose explosive power was calculated as 12,500 tons of TNT. Major Charles W. Sweeney and his crew, flying a B-29 bomber called Bock's Car, hit Nagasaki with Fat Man on August 9. Kokura Arsenal was their primary target, but it was covered with clouds. The Japanese emperor Hirohito ordered the Japanese people to surrender six days after Nagasaki was bombed. Robert Oppenheimer, soon to be referred as the father of the atomic bomb, reached into the Hindu scripture of the Bhagavad Gita and wrote, "Now I have become Death, the destroyer of worlds."

The Development of the Modern Computer

Breakthroughs in quantum mechanics in the 1920s have ushered in the electronic age. In the nineteenth century, an English scientist called Charles Babbage (1791–1871) received a large grant from Britain's Chancellor of the Exchequer (the British equivalent to the US Secretary of the Treasury) to build a computing machine. The problem was that he never completed his machine because, as long as he kept getting government money, he kept pursuing new ideas to develop the machine. Babbage conceived a machine that used punched cards. Nine years after Babbage's death, a young American civil servant, Herman Hollerith, introduced electricity into Babbage's punched-card machine and became the grandfather of IBM. Hollerith worked for the US Census. In 1880, hundreds of clerks tabulated the details of 50 million Americans by hand using quill pens. It took several years before the census's data became available; by then, the data was out of date.

In 1890, Hollerith invented a machine where one card for each of 63 million Americans had 288 places through which a hole could be punched. Contact completed an electric circuit when a hole appeared. A month after all returns were received in Washington, DC, the superintendent of the census was able to announce the total population of the United States with far more social statistics than were available before.

But Hollerith left the government and created his own private company, Tabulating Machine Company, and started charging the census bureau and other domestic and foreign clients. The US government complained that he was charging too much money. In 1914, with his company facing bankruptcy, Hollerith hired an executive from National Cash Register, Thomas W. Watson Sr. By 1929, before Hollerith's death, Watson had renamed the company International Business Machines (IBM). IBM developed punch-card desk calculators that physicist Stanislaw Ulam and Johnny used at Los Alamos in 1943–45 for the calculations of the A-bomb implosion. A person multiplying two sets of ten figures with pen and paper took about five minutes. The IBM punch-card desk calculator took ten to fifteen seconds. Soon, Johnny was looking for other methods to mathematize Los Alamos and was advised to try the IBM Harvard Mark I computer and the Bell Laboratory computer for one Los Alamos calculation in 1944 and found it quite useless. The punched cards in use at Los Alamos solved the problem in three weeks. After five weeks, the Harvard Mark I was still halfway through it in part for unnecessarily calculating each figure to eighteen decimal points.

Then in 1944, the first electronic computer, the Electronic Numerical Integrator and Computer (ENIAC) arrived a thousand times faster than any electricity-driven computer. ENIAC was born from a contract between the Ballistics Research Laboratory (BRL) at Aberdeen Proving Ground and the Moore School of Electrical Engineering at the University of Philadelphia. The father of the ENIAC was a young professor of physics at the Moore School called John Mauchly. In 1942, Mauchly wrote a memo proposing the building of a general-purpose electronic computer. The memo emphasized the enormous speed advantage to be gained by using digital electronics with no moving parts. Lieutenant Herman Goldstine of the US Army Ordnance Corps, who was the liaison between the US Army and the Moore School, liked the idea and asked Mauchly to write a formal proposal. In April 1943, the army contracted with the Moore School to build the ENIAC. Mauchly led the conceptual design while an electrical engineer, John Presper Eckert, led the hardware engineering on ENIAC. ENIAC could add 5,000 numbers or do 357 ten-digit multiplications in one second. But programming, initially accomplished with patch cords and switches and reprogramming, took days. ENIAC lacked an adequate stored memory. By 1944, Eckert and Mauchly had plans to design a second computer to be called Electronic Discrete Variable Computer (EDVAC) that would be a stored-program computer.

Later in 1944, von Neumann was introduced to the project by Goldstine who had met him at a railroad platform. On or about August 7, 1944, Goldstine took Johnny to see the ENIAC at Philadelphia. Then Johnny picked up Eckert and Mauchly's ideas and jumped blocks ahead of them. Johnny produced what was thought to be an internal document describing the EDVAC, the 101-page "First Draft of a Report on the EDVAC," dated June 30, 1945. Goldstine described this document as "the most important document ever written on computing and computers." Goldstine did something that would become very controversial: he removed any reference to Eckert or Mauchly and distributed copies of the document to a number of von Neumann's associates across the country. So the ideas came to be in the public domain. Mauchly and Eckert felt they had been cheated, and their bitterness towards Johnny grew over the years.

The ENIAC computer was formally accepted by the Philadelphia Ordnance District of the Army on June 30, 1946. But Johnny ensured that it completed abstruse computations at Los Alamos prior to it being disassembled and sent to Aberdeen. It took nine months of hard work to reassemble the seventeen thousand vacuum tubes at Aberdeen.

The electronic computer would be the most important machine of the second half of the twentieth century. Eckert and Mauchly hired patent attorneys to harvest their share of the profits. In March 1946, shortly after the ENIAC was announced, administrators of the Moore School did not like the idea of their employees applying for patents on equipment developed for US government projects. The Moore School would retain future patents on all projects. When Mauchly and Eckert were asked to sign a form consenting to this, they resigned. They started the Electronic Control Company. In 1946–47, working with the National Bureau of Standards, they created the Universal Automatic Computer (UNIVAC), and under contract with the Northrop Aircraft Company, they created the Binary Automatic Computer (BINAC)—a small computer for navigating airplanes. In 1948, they renamed their company

UNIVAC. The UNIVAC and the BINAC were the first computers to employ magnetic tape for data storage. In 1950, UNIVAC was acquired by the Remington Rand Corporation. John Mauchly died in January 1980 after spending his life with computers. For his work on ENIAC, John Mauchly was inducted, posthumously, into the National Inventors Hall of Fame. John Eckert received eighty-seven patents and numerous awards, including the Howard N. Potts and John Scott Medals (both shared with John Mauchly). President Lyndon B. Johnson presented him with the National Medal of Science in 1969. Eckert died in June 1995. I wanted to give a small tribute to these two great computer engineers.

Now let's go back to Johnny von Neumann. After World War II, he knew that work on large computers would be one of his most important projects. After WWII was over, Johnny wanted research scientists to use electronic computers to "jiggle" the planet and envisioned a three-hundred-thousand-dollar project for research and development of computers. The Institute for Advanced Studies (IAS) director, Aydelotte, in October 1945, recommended to the board of the IAS to contribute one hundred thousand dollars for Johnny's computer, "the most complex research instrument now in existence." The second portion would come from RCA, which was doing research on cathode ray tubes for the booming television industry. Johnny thought that the cathode ray tube would be the best technique for his computer's memory. By storing information on a cathode ray tube, he could get faster and more random access to a memory. The other two sponsors would be the US Army and the US Navy. Johnny got the generals and admirals enthusiastic about the potential applications of computers to military and naval operations. This included nuclear deterrence and the development of the hydrogen bomb as we shall see later.

Johnny's IAS colleagues were concerned that the army and navy would bring secrecy and nationalism, but Johnny was able to convince the generals and admirals to allow him to operate internationally and liberally (I'm surprised that he was able to do this during the Cold War!). He was able to share his progress reports of the IAS computer with 175 or so organizations around the world, resulting in the computer being copied and developed by the resident geniuses of each country. This allowed the computer technology to develop much faster than if his work had been done under a lid of secrecy by the small team of engineers at the IAS. This was the most important achievement of the IAS Computer Project.

The most important innovation was the development of the computer memory. The ENIAC needed a lengthy setup with switches and plugs; then it would do calculations at electronic speed. The Harvard Mark I could be fed instructions on a paper tape much faster, but the calculations would be a thousand times slower than the ENIAC. Goldstine and Johnny suggested a design that incorporated the best features of both, based on storing instructions as numbers in the computer's internal memory. The ideal memory would have unlimited capacity and unrestricted random access. This could never be achieved, but any improvement toward that goal resulted in significant development of the technology.

There were seven American clones of the IAS computer that reached full operation in 1952. Of these, the most important was the IBM 701. The 701 allowed IBM to dominate the world market.

In May–July 1946, Johnny negotiated a meteorological contract with the US Navy. This is credited with the beginning of modern meteorology. Meteorology presented problems that were nonlinear, multidimensional, and time dependent, with arbitrary initial and boundary conditions—the sort of problems computers were designed to solve. A team of meteorologists was put together, but the IAS computer was not ready yet, so the ENIAC computer at Aberdeen had to be hired for thirty-three days to run computations (it proved to be too slow, taking thirty-six hours to do a twenty-four-hour forecast). Research into meteorological forecasting met with limited success. But on November 25, 1950, there was a severe and unpredicted storm over the Eastern United States. The IAS team did 296,000 calculations on the IAS computer that showed that a twenty-four-hour forecast could be done in ten minutes. The US Weather Bureau and the armed forces got together and purchased an IBM 701 computer. On May 15, 1955, numerical weather forecasting began and has continued ever since in all advanced countries around the world with better and faster computers.

The amount of problems put on the IAS computer was disappointing. It needed too many hours of calculation to tackle complex problems. Other computers around the world were being developed faster than it.

After Johnny's death in February 1957, the IAS closed the Computer Project. The board passed a general motion that the IAS would, from then on, have no laboratories of any kind.

The Hydrogen Bomb

By the time of Japan's surrender in 1945, Johnny felt that there would be a war with the Soviet Union unless the United States maintained nuclear deterrence. Johnny believed that, by 1950, Russia would have discovered how to make nuclear bombs (Russia exploded its first atomic bomb in 1949). Johnny hoped that Russia could be contained with deterrence more thoughtfully and resolutely than deterrence had been enforced against Nazi Germany in the 1930s. Johnny's military activity and political opinions in 1946–49 were shaped by these convictions.

Johnny spent two months a year at Los Alamos. In 1945, he analyzed the paths that had been taken by the atomic explosions at Hiroshima and Nagasaki. He concluded from his calculations that nuclear bombs could be made terribly more efficient rather easily. So nuclear fission, and later fusion, would provide the weapons that would keep the peace.

In mid-1945, the Soviets had started a nuclear research effort. German nuclear scientists in Soviet-occupied East Germany were taken to the Soviet Union and put to work not in prison camps but in comfortable laboratory conditions. So were captured German scientists who had worked on the V-2 rockets. Laventy Beria, chief of the secret police, was in charge of the Soviet Union's nuclear research. Beria had a reputation of being a most dangerous man.

Johnny's military objective was to help America obtain a more powerful bomb. After WWII, most scientists were leaving Los Alamos to teach at their home universities. By late 1946, there were only eight theoretical physicists left at Los Alamos. Johnny would visit for a month at a time and was becoming the most admired figure at the mesa.

At a meeting where Johnny was a participant at Los Alamos in 1946, it was recommended that "a detailed calculation" be conducted to study mathematically the progress of a hydrogen bomb (the Super) explosion. The result was a classified project called Hippo. Hippo found that the explosion at Hiroshima was the equivalent of thirteen thousand tons of TNT (thirteen kilotons) while the implosion at Nagasaki had released twenty-one kilotons. The explosion at Nagasaki had done a lot less damage, but from Hippo, Johnny learned where to place the bombs and what secondary factors to consider. Johnny was starting to realize that someday, nuclear bombs would have to be lighter so they could be carried by missiles, artillery shells, mines, or torpedoes.

On August 29, 1949, as Johnny had predicted, the Soviet Union exploded a nuclear bomb. The United States had aircraft flying high in the skies over the Soviet Union on patrol with protruding filters to pick up nuclear debris. In late August 1949, the filters picked up such debris. After three weeks of examination, President Truman announced that the USSR had a nuclear device nicknamed Joe 1. A debate started as to whether the United States should proceed with the development of the Super bomb, or the H-bomb. The strongest advocates of the H-bomb were Edward Teller and Ernest Lawrence. In early 1946, Teller presented his proposed design to a secret committee of thirty-one scientists, including Johnny (the same meeting that produced the HIPPO project mentioned earlier). The committee concluded that Teller's design would probably work but require a lot of resources. At the time, nobody wanted to spend a lot of money and resources on something like the H-bomb. After August 1949, Teller barnstormed through Washington lobbying so his bomb would be given the highest priority.

Oppenheimer and Enrico Fermi argued that it would destroy millions of innocent lives and the release of radioactivity would render large areas of the planet uninhabitable for a long time. Oppenheimer argued that he was not sure that "the miserable thing can work, nor that it can be gotten to the target except by oxcart." He proposed the improvement of America's existing atomic bombs. He did not believe that computers would be ready to do the calculations required for the H-bomb. But Johnny agreed with Teller that "if the super can be made, it should be made by America." He knew that computers would be able to do the necessary calculations to develop the H-bomb. Oppenheimer doubted that the Russians would start researching the H-bomb right away. Johnny was sure that they had already started. Today, we know that Sakharov was researching Russian's H-bomb since 1948.

In January 1950, President Truman directed the Atomic Energy Commission (AEC) to continue work on all kinds of atomic weapons, including "the so-called hydrogen or super bomb."

Scientists began to return to Los Alamos, including Fermi and Bethe. Fermi, like a good soldier, considered that once the president had made a decision, it was not the scientists' place to inject their opinions. Bethe confessed that he was hoping to prove that the Super would not work but found that everybody at Los Alamos was gung ho about creating the H-bomb. For a time, calculations done by Dr. Stanislaw Ulam and Dr. C. J. Everett showed that Teller's original design would not work (fortunately, Klaus Fuchs had reported this original design to the Soviets). Finally, between January and March 1951, Teller and Ulam managed to refine the design of the bomb, and in May 1951, the so-called George shot lighted "the first small thermonuclear flame on Earth."

Development of the H-bomb proceeded until the Mike shot at Eniwetok in November 1952 exploded with an equivalent force of ten megatons of TNT (almost a thousand times more powerful that the Hiroshima bomb). The Mike device required a building full of refrigeration units to maintain the liquid deuterium in its proper state before the explosion. It could not be transported by airplane. But by the Castle shot in March 1954, the fifteen-megaton device could be dropped by an airplane.

The Soviet Union exploded a tiny thermonuclear device, perhaps five hundred kilotons, on August 12, 1953. Probably its small yield was the result of Fuchs reporting only the initial Teller ideas of 1946 that did not work (Klaus Fuchs's espionage activities were discovered in 1949 and arrested in England after the cracking of Soviet ciphers known as the Venona project. He confessed in 1950 and was sentenced to fourteen years in prison. Released in 1959, he was allowed to emigrate to East Germany where he resumed a scientific career. He died in East Germany in 1988.) In 1955, Sakharov produced the equivalent of the Teller-Ulam bomb.

Johnny was satisfied that the United States had won the race for developing the H-bomb before the Soviets. But he still wrote to Admiral Lewis Strauss, a trustee of the Institute of Advanced Studies, that a confrontation between the United States and the USSR was very probable. The United States had to flash a message to the USSR leaders that, if they dared to engage in war, they would be nuked to death, and although shattered, the United States would win the war.

In November 1952, Dwight Eisenhower was elected president of the United States. He appointed Lewis Strauss as special assistant for atomic energy matters and, later, as chairman of the Atomic Energy Commission. Eisenhower also brought in Donald A. Quarles, first as assistant secretary of defense for research and development and, later, as secretary of the Air Force. Quarles had Trevor Gardner as special assistant to the secretary of the air force. All three of these men were fans of Johnny.

After Truman endorsed the development of the Super bomb in January 1950, the military services started recruiting "hard nuts such as Johnny instead of gentle poets such as Oppenheimer." Johnny was appointed to the Weapons Systems Evaluation Group (WSEG) and to the Armed Forces Special Weapons Project (AFSWP). But Johnny was appalled and exasperated by the military bureaucracy he found. He felt that the Atomic Energy Commission and his fellow scientists had not explained to the military how easy it would be to kill millions of people with nuclear weapons. He described the relations between the AEC and the services as "chaotic" with lack of information in places where it should have been available and misunderstandings and misdirections of effort. It took Johnny's diplomacy and growing influence to work in this environment.

Between 1951 and 1952, Johnny was appointed as consultant to the Central Intelligence Agency; member of the General Advisory Committee (GAC), a committee of top scientists that advised the AEC; consultant to Lawrence and Teller's new rival laboratory at Livermore; and member of the scientific advisory board to the US Air Force. Robert Oppenheimer had been the chairman of the GAC for five years. Although Oppenheimer opposed the development of the hydrogen bomb (the Super) and

Johnny disagreed with him, the two men were able to work very well together. Oppenheimer had treated rudely Lewis Strauss when Strauss was a trustee of the IAS. When in 1953, Strauss became Eisenhower's chairman of the AEC, he proceeded to get rid of Oppenheimer. Eventually, an inquiry in 1954 by the AEC instigated by Strauss resulted in Oppenheimer being stripped of his security clearance. This happened during the McCarthy era when US Senator Joseph McCarthy from Wisconsin was conducting a witch hunt for people with links to the communist party. Robert Oppenheimer had had some sympathy for the communists in the 1930s and, during the war, had been asked by a leftist friend to provide classified information to the Soviets. Although he refused to comply, Oppenheimer had failed to report this incident in a timely manner to security officials. This incident was twisted by Strauss's lawyer to make Oppenheimer appear as someone who could not be trusted with America's nuclear secrets. But Johnny, despite being to the right of most scientists, did not play any part in McCarthyism. During Oppenheimer's hearing, he organized a group of witnesses for Oppenheimer—those who disagreed with Oppenheimer's opposition to the Super bomb but did not consider him to be a security threat. Despite this, Johnny managed to maintain excellent relations with Lewis Strauss until his death.

In 1954, Johnny became chairman of the most important committee that advised the secretary of the air force on all large military rocket programs, the Strategic Missiles Evaluation Group. This committee was unofficially known as the von Neumann Committee. Johnny's combination of being powerful and productive in science and mathematics mixed with strong practicality gave him great credibility with military officers, engineers, industrialists, and scientists. He was the highest advisory figure in nuclear missilery, and his advice was taken very seriously.

The first question asked of Johnny's nuclear weapons panels was, what would be the maximum yield of a hydrogen bomb that could be carried by a B-52 bomber? Johnny's panel answered that they forecasted that a B-52 could carry a twenty-megaton bomb (twenty thousand tons of TNT).

The second question for Johnny's panel was if it would be possible to get a bomb weighing about three thousand pounds that could be carried in an Atlas missile that could destroy everything within five hundred yards. Johnny's panel replied that it would be possible to develop a bomb that weighed less than three thousand pounds with a yield of two megatons that would destroy everything within 3.2–4.5 miles. Eventually, planners compromised to build the Atlas missile to carry a one-megaton bomb that would destroy everything within two miles.

The von Neumann committee later reported (1) that it was possible to build a rocket-powered ballistic missile that would carry a nuclear warhead across a quarter of the world and deliver it with accuracy, (2) that the Soviets may be some years ahead of America in this field, and (3) that new management techniques would be needed so that America could catch up. U.S. Air Force General Bernard Schriever, head of the USAF Western Development Division of the Air Research and Development Command, who worked closely with Johnny's committee, developed what is now called the systems management, widely adopted in the industry. The creation of the intercontinental ballistic missile (ICBM) fleet in less than eight years was a great feat for General Schriever. Another innovation that was instrumental in the timely development of the ICBM fleet was industrialists Ramo and Wooldridge of the von Neumann committee formed the Ramo-Wooldridge Group to provide what the weapons industry called general systems engineering and technical direction (GSETD). Eventually, Ramo-Wooldridge became a company called TRW, now a major defense contractor.

Six American missile systems were born from the recommendations of the von Neumann committee. These missiles guarded the peace from the 1950s to the end of the Cold War. Three were intercontinental ballistic missiles (Atlas, Titan, and Minuteman). Two were intermediate range (Thor and Jupiter). Polaris was submarine launched. Jupiter was an army missile system.

In the summer of 1954, Strauss became concerned that Johnny was involved in too many activities simultaneously and convinced him to accept an appointment from President Eisenhower to be one of America's five atomic energy commissioners. Strauss then coached Johnny on how to respond to questions during the ratification process by a joint committee of Congress. Johnny's appointment to the Atomic Energy Commission would have been from 1955 to 1959, but it was tragically cut short by cancer.

Johnny continued to be involved in many scientific areas that interested him. He worked by day in the AEC. In the evening, scientists of the many scientific fields that interested Johnny came to visit him. His wife, Klari, acted as night secretary. She entertained his visitors and passed them to him one at a time. Even during sleep, Johnny was working. Often, he would go to sleep with an unsolved problem in his mind and wake up at 3:00 a.m. with the answer. Then he would call one of his associates to discuss it. One of the requirements when Johnny hired associates was they could not be upset if he called them any time of the day or night. Even after only a few hours of sleep, Johnny would go to work as if he had had a full night's sleep.

One of the last projects in which he worked until his death was *The Computer and the Brain* for his intended Silliman lectures. Johnny thought that the human brain was much slower than his computers to perform complex mathematical calculations, but the brain could do many other tasks that computers could not do, such as visual recognition, imagination, and judgment. Johnny believed that "when we talk mathematics we may be discussing a secondary language built on the prime language truly used by the central nervous system." Johnny wanted to find that language.

In 1956, Johnny informed the IAS that after his term with the AEC, he would work as professor at large with the University of California. This was the best way for him to launch his new mathematics since IAS scientists had a vested interest in preserving the "old" mathematics. Because he had lost income while in government service, IBM would be bringing him additional funds by taking patents in his name for innovations he had suggested to them.

In August 1955, Strauss was in Switzerland for an international meeting about radiation diseases. He received a cable from Johnny that said that he had been diagnosed with "a very probably benign 'giant cell' tumor on left shoulder clavicular bone. Recommended operation not absolutely necessary but without unnecessary delay." At first, Strauss did not understand the seriousness of this diagnosis, but when he discussed it with some of the world's great cancer experts who were in the meeting, they advised—to his horror—that a giant cell tumor on the left-shoulder clavicular bone was very likely to be cancer. Johnny's cancer probably started in the pancreas and had spread through his bloodstream and bones. Johnny possibly did not notice the pain while concentrating on his work.

Johnny launched himself into a great frenzy of activity to finish the projects he had started, but by November 1955, he was in a wheelchair. In January 1955, Johnny had to be hospitalized but came out, in a wheelchair, to receive a special Medal of Freedom from President Eisenhower. He told the President "I wish I could be around long enough to deserve this honor." Eisenhower replied, "You will be with us for a long time, we need you."

When his daughter, Marina, then twenty years old, decided to get married straight after finishing her bachelor's degree *summa cum laude*, Johnny was worried. He thought that an early marriage would derail an academic career (something very possible for a woman in the 1950s). But years later, Dr. Marina von Neumann Whitman became a member of President Nixon's council of economic advisors, the first woman to receive such an honor. Johnny was able to attend Marina's engagement party in a wheelchair but had to go back to the hospital before her marriage. Strauss and many military officers and other great and important people visited Johnny frequently in the hospital. In case Johnny talked in his sleep, soldiers were posted in his room to prevent unauthorized persons from listening to classified information. It appears that Johnny did hallucinate in his sleep but did so in Hungarian.

Johnny died on February 8, 1957; he had turned fifty-three little over a month earlier. He was buried in Princeton Cemetery beside his mother's grave. Johnny's wife, Klara, committed suicide in 1963 by walking into the ocean.

His daughter, Dr. Marina von Neumann Whitman, had a distinguished career as an economist. Among her many achievements, after serving as a member of President Nixon's council of economic advisors, she served as vice president and chief economist and, later, as vice president and group executive for public affairs for General Motors Corporation. She is currently a professor of business administration and public policy at the University of Michigan at Ann Arbor. Johnny must be immensely proud of her. This relatively short chapter attempted to summarize the life of a great scientist but could not mention all his achievements. Who knows what incredible developments Johnny would have produced if he had lived a few more years!

Jonas Salk
The Man Who Conquered Polio

I was born in 1954, the year that Jonas Salk conducted his trials of his polio vaccine on over a million children (polio pioneers). Thanks to him, no one in my family suffered the effects of polio.

Jonas Salk is one of the most venerated medical scientists of the twentieth century. For that reason, I will give him a humble tribute in this chapter of my book. The short and very readable biography *Jonas Salk: Beyond the Microscope* by Victoria Sherrow was my primary source.

Poliomyelitis epidemics used to strike people in the United States during summertime. In 1921, a young politician named Franklin Delano Roosevelt was stricken by polio and left with his legs permanently paralyzed. The virus enters the body by nose or mouth and travels to the intestines where it incubates. Five to thirty-one days later, the virus reaches the nervous system where it multiplies and destroys the nerve tissue. At this point, the disease becomes spinal or bulbar (involving the last four or five cranial nerves). The spinal form affects the limbs. The bulbar form affects the lungs so that the patient cannot breathe. These patients had to be placed in iron lungs to help them breathe; some would spend decades in these iron lungs.

Jonas Salk was the son of Russian-Jewish immigrants who, although lacking formal education, encouraged their children to study and work hard to succeed in life. Jonas Salk was the first member of his family to go to college. He entered City College of New York, originally intending to study law. But curiosity led him to enroll in a chemistry class where he was captivated by "the magic of nature" and was excited about science. He decided to switch his major to chemistry then entered medical school and become a medical researcher. He went to New York University Medical School. There in 1938, he began working with microbiologist Thomas Francis Jr. who was researching a vaccine for influenza. Salk spent a year researching influenza. After completing his medical degree and his internship, Dr. Salk returned to do research on the influenza virus with Dr. Thomas Francis at the University of Michigan to develop an influenza vaccine.

At the outbreak of World War II, the Armed Forces Epidemiological Board asked Thomas Francis to develop a vaccine against different strains of influenza, especially influenza A. During World War I, influenza had killed over 550,000Americans—44,000 of them in the military. Francis asked Salk to join him, and the board agreed to let Salk work on flu vaccine instead of serving in the US Army Medical Corps. Jonas had married Donna Lindsay upon receiving his medical degree in 1939. He and Donna travelled to Michigan where they rented a small apartment in an old farmhouse. Donna found a job as a social worker. Jonas, in addition to laboratory research, taught classes in epidemiology. An epidemic of type A influenza occurred in 1943 and Francis's team used this strain in their vaccine. They developed a killed-virus vaccine. Salk had developed a blood test to calculate the amount of antibody in the blood. With Salk's test, the team found a direct relationship between the level of antibodies and the amount of resistance to new attacks of influenza. Their tests showed that the killed-virus vaccine could stimulate the production of antibody levels as high as those produced by the flu itself.

By 1943, Francis had organized field trials to test their influenza vaccine on human volunteers. During the winter of 1943–1944, twenty-five thousand people participated in these trials. Results showed that killed-virus influenza vaccine worked. Salk coauthored several scientific articles about the influenza research and field tests with Francis and other members of the team that were published in the *American Journal of Public Health*, the *Journal of Immunology*, and the *Journal of Clinical Investigations*. Salk had been appointed to the United States Army Influenza Commission in 1943. Between 1945 and 1947, he spent weeks in Europe, with the temporary rank of army major, conducting studies on influenza and setting up laboratories in Germany where US troops were still stationed. Those laboratories were designed to diagnose influenza quickly to prevent a postwar epidemic. The influenza epidemic of 1919 did not recur.

After the war, Salk was eager to run his own lab but was not sure what disease he would investigate. It so happened that the National Foundation for Infantile Paralysis was actively looking for scientists to research a cure for polio. This organization had been founded by Franklin Delano Roosevelt after he was left paralyzed by polio. He purchased a thermal pool in rural Warm Springs, Georgia, which he turned into a combination vacation resort and treatment center for polio survivors. In 1927, FDR's law partner and friend, Basil O'Connor, suggested that Warm Springs be run as a charitable foundation supported by grants and donations. O'Connor became the new foundation's first director. In 1938, the Warm Springs Foundation became the National Foundation for Infantile Paralysis (NFIP). Americans were urged to give dimes or whatever they could afford to fight polio. In 1938, the foundation raised $1.8 million. Millions of dollars were raised during the 1940s. In 1941, O'Connor declared that they intended to "completely eradicate the disease." The NFIP grants financed a great deal of basic research in viruses and polio. But by 1947, there was still no cure for polio.

In 1935, two polio vaccines had been tested. At the New York Health Department, Dr. Maurice Brodie and Dr. William Park made a killed-virus vaccine. In Philadelphia, Dr. John Kolmer made a vaccine using live but weakened viruses. The Park-Brodie vaccine was administered to nine thousand people, but three test subjects were paralyzed and one died. The Kolmer vaccine was administered to ten thousand people; nine children and one adult were left paralyzed and five children died. The researchers concluded that these vaccines may have caused the polios. An Australian virologist, Sir McFarlane Burnet, had an explanation based on his research. There were different kinds of polioviruses, which meant that the body must be exposed to each of them before it can make antibodies against them. These failed tests haunted researchers. How many types of polioviruses were there, and how did they enter the body—through the nose, mouth, or other routes? But by the 1940s, more scientists thought that a safe vaccine was feasible. Salk favored a preventive vaccine since observation showed that people who survived polio did not get it again. They must have become immune.

In 1947, the University of Pittsburg contacted Dr. Jonas Salk. Dr. William McEllroy, dean of the College of Medicine, offered Salk office and laboratory space in the city-owned hospital next to the college. Salk's new lab consisted of two rooms in the basement of the municipal hospital. Dr. Harry Weaver, director of research for the NFIP, wanted to find out how many types of polioviruses there were. He recommended that the NFIP fund a program to count and type polioviruses. Then scientists would determine if each type required separate immunity or whether antibodies that fought one virus could also combat other polioviruses. Salk saw in this project an opportunity to learn more about immunology and expand his laboratory.

The NFIP gave Salk a grant and chose the Pittsburg Virus Research Laboratory as one of the four typing teams. The project was expected to last three years. Each team had a part of the project. The NFIP committee overseeing the typing program consisted of Thomas Francis, who isolated the type I virus; Armstrong Lansing, who found a type II strain; and Dr. John Kessel who identified the type III strain. Another member was Dr. Albert Sabin, a pediatrician who had been working on a polio vaccine at the University of Cincinnati. Salk wanted to infect monkeys with unknown virus types. He wanted to type the viruses by measuring the blood antibodies that resulted from exposure to different strains in order to determine which known virus the antibodies worked against. Sabin criticized this approach. The NFIP committee approved a different approach to infect monkeys with known virus types and then test unknown viruses in these monkeys and their blood. The idea was to determine if the strains were type I, II, or III. The committee also wanted researchers to calculate the amount of virus needed to cause infection. Salk worked overtime using both approaches. As a result, he had the job done in one year. The work of the next two years merely confirmed the results of the first year.

In 1949, a team from Boston Children's Hospital was able to grow Lansing (type II) polioviruses in human embryonic tissues. The three scientists Dr. John Enders, Fred Robbins, and Tom Weller received the 1954 Nobel Prize in Physiology or Medicine for inciting "a restless activity in the virus laboratories the world over." Polio researchers could now grow large amounts of poliovirus for their studies. There was no longer a need to wait until infected monkeys would die to obtain viruses from their spinal cords. For decades, scientists had not been able to grow polioviruses in anything but nervous tissue, which can cause allergic reactions or even death. Now researchers could hope to develop a vaccine without nervous tissue.

After the Pittsburg team finished typing viruses, Salk was working on a polio vaccine. In 1951, Basil O'Connor asked Salk to conduct more research. O'Connor's daughter, Bettyman, a mother of five, had been stricken with polio in 1950. In 1951, the NFIP was making plans to develop polio vaccines. The name of the Committee on Typing and Strains was changed to the Committee on Immunization. The NFIP gave Salk more funding, and he increased his team to fifty people and purchased more laboratory equipment. The core group of Salk's research team included microbiologist Dr. Julius Younger, Dr. L. James Lewis, Major Byron L. Barnett, and zoologist Elsie N. Ward who specialized in growing and maintaining live virus cultures. Australian Dr. Percival Bazaley was an expert in making large quantities of pharmaceutical materials. Other members were Dr. Donald Wegemer, Dr. Ulrich Krech, and Francis Yurochko. Julius Younger and Elsie Ward were assigned the task of growing polioviruses in nonnervous tissue (tissue from organs outside the brain and spinal cord). Their research found that monkey kidney was the best medium for virus growth. Younger found that, by adding trypsin—a digestive enzyme produced in the pancreas to the tissue—caused it to break down into distinct cells where viruses grow. The result was that larger quantities of virus could grow on the same amount of tissue. The Pittsburg lab was able to grow large quantities of different poliovirus strains. In addition, Younger developed a rapid color test that indicated the presence of antibodies in tissue.

There was debate among scientists: Some, like Dr. Albert Sabin, argued that a live-virus vaccine was needed so people were exposed to an actual infection in order to trigger production of antibodies. Salk favored a killed-virus vaccine. He had evidence that a killed-virus vaccine could produce immunity; he and Thomas Francis had proved it with their flu vaccine. He used formalin, a solution of 37 percent formaldehyde, for "cooking the virus"—that is, exposing the poliovirus to different amounts of formalin at different temperatures to kill the viruses. In 1952, Salk obtained permission to test his killed-virus vaccine on seventy-nine children at the D. T. Watson Home for Crippled Children (now the Watson Institute) in Pennsylvania. He injected his vaccine into the forearms of his young volunteers; nobody became sick. Seven months later, he administered the volunteers a final immunization shot called a booster. Tests done on the children's blood showed higher levels of antibodies after the final injection.

Salk then gave the vaccine to volunteers who had not had polio—including himself, his staff, his wife, and his three children. All developed antibodies and no adverse reactions to the vaccine. Then, in 1954, national testing began on one million children, aged six to nine, who were known as polio pioneers. Half received the vaccine and half a placebo. In April 1955, results were announced on television: the vaccine worked, and it was safe and effective. In the two years before the vaccine became widely available, the average number of polio cases in the United States was 45,000. By 1962, the number had shrunk to 910. Salk became an international hero. He spent the 1950s refining the vaccine and establishing the scientific principles behind it. Salk never patented the vaccine nor did he earn any money from it. He wanted it distributed as widely as possible. President Eisenhower presented Salk and Basil O'Connor with the US Medal of Merit. Eisenhower was moved to tears as he expressed gratitude that his grandchildren could be protected from polio.

The success of the vaccine got Salk a great amount of publicity. He received pleas from top manufacturers to endorse their products. Hollywood studios wanted to make a movie about his life, but he refused, saying such films were best made after their subjects died. People sent him cash and gifts, including cars; Salk announced that he was donating all of these to the NFIP. The media called him "the man who conquered polio." All this publicity regretfully alienated Jonas Salk from the scientific community. Some scientists called him a "glory hound."

In 1957, Albert Sabin began testing an oral form of vaccine using inactivated (attenuated) live virus. Instead of administering it by injection, Sabin's vaccine was taken by mouth on a lump of sugar. This vaccine became available for use in 1963. The two vaccines were used throughout the world. Eventually, the Sabin vaccine was used almost exclusively in the United States until the year 2000 when the Centers for Disease Control advised physicians to switch to the killed-virus vaccine, except in very special cases. The Sabin vaccine had caused several cases of polio each year. In 1960, there were 2,525 cases of polio in the United States. By 1965, there were 61. Between 1980 and 19990, there was an average of 8 per year—most of these induced by vaccination. There were no cases of polio by the wild poliovirus since 1979. In 1994, polio was declared eradicated in all of the Americas.

Jonas Salk was nominated for the Nobel Prize in Medicine or Physiology, but incredibly, he did not receive it. He was also turned down for membership in the National Academy of Sciences, probably as a result of the hostility that his fame produced on some scientists.

The Salk Institute

Salk tried to go back to work with minimal publicity but the public and journalists would follow all his activities. In 1958, a survey found that Jonas Salk was one of the two best-known American scientists. The other was physicist Robert Oppenheimer, the father of the atomic bomb.

In 1957, Salk was commonwealth professor of experimental medicine but was frustrated by the amount of time he had to spend on administrative duties. He was interested in cancer and multiple sclerosis. Both illnesses were highly complex and would require decades of research and collaboration with many scientists.

Salk envisioned a scientific institution with brilliant scientists working on many projects in a stimulating research community. He decided that since he could not find such an institution, why not create one himself? Basil O'Connor offered financial support for the institute, and $20 million of the initial funding was provided by the National Foundation/March of Dimes. Other funding came from the National Institutes of Health, private individuals, and organizations.

In 1960, Salk resigned from the University of Pittsburg to dedicate himself to the design of the institute. He had considered locating the institute on the University of Pittsburg campus, but the university officials wanted some control over the institute, and Salk wanted autonomy. In 1959, Salk met Mayor Charles Dail of San Diego, himself crippled by polio. Mayor Dail asked the city to donate land along the Torrey Pines mesa in La Jolla, near the University of California at San Diego. Salk wanted buildings and surroundings to "evoke and inspire creativity." A famous architect, Philadelphia architect and artist Lois I. Kahn, designed the buildings set on twenty-six acres overlooking the ocean. Construction began in 1962. The design, innovative yet simple, is considered an architectural masterpiece.

The Salk Institute for Biological Studies was officially inaugurated as a nonprofit organization in 1963 with Salk as its first president. Since the buildings were still under construction, people began working from temporary facilities. In 1965, Salk resigned as president to serve as director. The core building was completed in 1967. The institute attracted some of the brightest scientists in the world. Resident fellows and faculty members included Nobel laureates and members of prestigious scientific societies, such as the National Academy of Sciences and the Royal Academy of London. By 1968, 140 people were working at the institute—most of them in research. Salk devoted himself to the study of multiple sclerosis, cancer, and autoimmune diseases. He continued to work sixteen to eighteen hours a day, six days a week. Salk was also writing and teaching. He was appointed adjunct professor in health sciences at the University of California at San Diego.

In 1968, Donna and Jonas Salk divorced. Donna did not enjoy the public attention and numerous public events required of her famous husband. After the divorce, she remained at San Diego and resumed her career as a social worker. Jonas remarried in 1970 to French-born artist Françoise Gilot. Gilot had studied law, philosophy, and literature, as well as art. She had lived with the famous Spanish artist Pablo Picasso, with whom she had two children.

In 1972, Salk changed his role at the institute. Although he retained the title of director, he was no longer involved in administrative duties. He devoted himself to research and humanitarian activities. In 1975, his title at the institute changed to founding director.

Between 1972 and 1984, Salk published several books blending his scientific and philosophical thinking. The first book, *Man Unfolding* (1972), discussed ways in which science affects the larger society. This book has been included in reading lists for college philosophy courses. One of his books was written with his younger son Jonathan who studied child development at Harvard University and earned a degree in anthropology from Stanford University. The book, *World Population and Human Values: A New Reality*, was published in 1981 and describes population pattern throughout history and discusses values to maximize human potential while adjusting to changes in the world's population. His other books are *The Survival of the Wisest* (1973), *How Like an Angel: Biology and the Nature of Man* (1975), and *Anatomy of Reality: Merging of Intuition and Reason* (1984).

In 1977, President Jimmy Carter awarded him the Presidential Medal of Freedom, the nation's highest civilian award. At the ceremony, President Carter said, "Because of his tireless work, untold hundreds of thousands who might have been crippled are sound in body today." Salk received this award the same day that the late civil rights leader, the Reverend Dr. Martin Luther King Jr. assassinated in 1968, was honored. Salk paid tribute to Dr. King when he accepted his own medal. He said, "The ultimate freedoms we seek, freedom from exploitation and oppression." He continued to say, "Without freedom from oppression and from disease, the pursuit of happiness has little meaning."

In the late 1980s, Jonas Salk studied HIV/AIDS for six years. The Salk Institute made important contributions in the fields of genetics, immunology, and neurology among others. Neuroscience, a major interest of Jonas Salk, became the major focus of the institute.

Salk cofounded a biotechnology company called Immune Corporation that would produce and market a vaccine against HIV if and when it was developed. In 1989, the company produced HIV immunotherapeutic, an immune-based therapy based on Salk's research. This was not a true vaccine but a treatment to delay or prevent AIDS symptoms in people already infected.

In 1985, President Ronald Reagan declared May 6 as Dr. Jonas E. Salk Day. In 1995, the March of Dimes initiated an award in Salk's honor. The March of Dimes Prize in Developmental Biology is given annually to a researcher or scientific team who contributed significantly to the study of birth defects. The prize includes a medal and $250,000. In 2006, the US Postal Office issued a sixty-three-cent stamp in honor of Jonas Salk, medical scientist.

Jonas Salk died on June 23, 1995, of congestive heart failure at the age of eighty. A special issue of *Time* magazine dated March 29, 1999, featured Salk's picture on the cover along with Albert Einstein and Sigmund Freud. *Time* listed Salk as one of the century's one hundred most important scientists and thinkers.

Watson and Crick
The Search for the Double Helix

In the introduction to James Watson's *The Double Helix*, Sylvia Nascar, author of *A Beautiful Mind*—the story of mathematician John Nash—said about Watson, "The former radio Quiz Kid and ornithologist from Chicago had gone to Cambridge, England, in search of glory, girls, and the secret of genes—not necessarily in that order." And in his book, which he originally intended to title *Honest Jim* but fortunately was advised by his attorney Alan Schwartz to change the title to *The Double Helix*, James Watson does mention many times, with great sense of humor, his interest in beautiful young women. Those comments got him in trouble later in his life, but that's a different story. The discovery of the structure of the molecule of DNA (deoxyribonucleic acid, a self-replicating material present in nearly all living organisms as the main constituent of chromosomes; it is the carrier of genetic information) has been described as one of the most important scientific feats of the twentieth century.

When James Dewey Watson went to Cambridge University Cavendish Laboratory, he was hoping that the secret of genes could be solved "without learning any chemistry." As an undergraduate at the University of Chicago, he managed to avoid taking any courses in chemistry or physics, "which looked even of medium difficulty."

As a child, James was fascinated by birds. He appeared on *Quiz Kids*, a popular radio show that challenged smart kids to answer questions. He enrolled at the University of Chicago at the age of fifteen. Reading theoretical physicist's Erwin Schrodinger's book *What Is Life?* in 1946 changed his professional plans from ornithology (the study of birds) to genetics. He graduated from the University of Chicago in 1947 with a degree in zoology. He attended Indiana University from 1947 to 1950, earning a PhD in zoology at age twenty-two. He began his PhD research in Salvador Luria's laboratory at Indiana University and got to meet Max Debruck. Luria, an Italian-trained microbiologist, and Delbruck shared a Nobel Prize on the Luria-Delbruck experiment concerning the nature of genetic mutations. Luria and Delbruck were among the leaders of a group of researchers who were using viruses that infect bacteria, called bacteriophages; the group was referred to as the Phage Group. Watson became a working scientist within this Phage Group.

Watson went to the University of Copenhagen to do postdoctoral studies under biochemist Herman Kalckar. His PhD supervisor at Indiana University, Salvador Luria, shared Watson's dislike for chemistry and hoped that, under Kalckar's civilized company, Watson could learn "the necessary tools to do chemistry research, without needing to react against the profit-oriented organic chemists." Kalckar was working in the enzymatic synthesis of nucleic acids, and he wanted to use phages as an experimental system. But Watson was interested in exploring the structure of DNA and was not interested in Kalckar's work. He spent only part of the year with Kalckar and the rest of his time in Copenhagen doing experiments with microbial physiologist Ole Maaloe, a member of the Phage Group.

Although Watson was not interested in the work of Kalckar, he accompanied him to a meeting in Italy where Watson attended a presentation by Maurice Wilkins about x-ray diffraction data for DNA. Watson was hooked. Wilkins's x-ray diffraction pictures suggested that DNA could be arising from a crystalline substance. When the structure of DNA was known, scientists would be in a better position to understand how genes worked. Now, Watson was excited about chemistry. He knew that genes could crystallize, so they must have a crystalline structure that could be solved. Watson tried to engage Wilkins, hoping to be able to join him in his work on DNA, but Wilkins kept his distance (despite Wilkins taking a brief interest in Watson's sister, Elizabeth, who had accompanied him to the meeting in Naples). Luria helped Watson get a new postdoctoral research project at the Cavendish Laboratory in Cambridge University, England, in 1952.

At Cambridge, Watson met Francis Crick, a physicist who was studying a doctorate in molecular biology. Watson started his book *The Double Helix*, describing Crick: "he talked louder and faster than anyone else and, when he laughed, his location within Cavendish was obvious." And he described the relationship between Francis Crick and Sir Lawrence Bragg: "conversations with Crick frequently upset Sir Lawrence Bragg, and the sound of his voice was often sufficient to make Bragg move to a safer room. Only infrequently would he come to tea in the Cavendish, since it meant enduring Crick's booming voice over the tea room. Even then Bragg was not completely safe. On two occasions the corridor outside his office was flooded with water pouring out of a laboratory in which Crick was working. Francis, with his interest in theory, had neglected to fasten securely the rubber tubing around his suction cups." (When Sir Lawrence read the manuscript of *The Double Helix*, he was furious. His wife had to calm him down.) But in his other book, *Avoid Boring People*, Watson mentioned that during World War II, Crick, then a physicist, worked for the Admiralty and joined the high-powered working to invent countermeasures against German magnetic mines. His boss, nuclear physicist Harrie Massey, assigned Francis in 1943 the project of combating the German Navy's latest innovation, a new class of minesweepers (Sperrbrechers) that had five hundred tons of electromagnets in their bows, designed to trigger magnetic mines from a safe distance. Crick designed a mine that would not explode until the Sperrbrechers passed directly over it. "Over a hundred Sperrbrechers were sent to the bottom of the ocean." But after the war, Francis Crick decided not to pursue a career in physics and switched to biology.

In 1951, the chemist Linus Pauling, considered by many the as world's best chemist, published a model for the amino acid alpha helix, a discovery from Linus's work in x-ray crystallography and molecular model building. Watson and Crick realized that Linus Pauling's discovery was a product of common sense, not of complicated mathematical reasoning. According to Watson, "the key to Linus' success was his reliance on the simple laws of structural chemistry. The alpha helix had not been found by only staring at x-ray pictures; the essential trick, instead, was to ask which atoms like to sit next to each other." Linus's main working tools had been a set of molecular models resembling toys of preschool children. Watson and Crick figured they could solve DNA in the same way. They decided "to construct a set of molecular models and begin to play."

Maurice Wilkins was born on December 15, 1916, at Pangaroa, New Zealand. His father was a medical doctor. His family moved to Birmingham, England, when he was six. He studied physics at Saint John's College, Cambridge, and in 1940, he received his PhD in physics at the University of Birmingham. During World War II, he developed improved radar screens at Birmingham and then worked on isotope separation in the Manhattan Project at the University of California, Berkeley, for two years. After the war, he was disgusted with the dropping of two atomic bombs on civilian centers in Japan. He decided to go into biology. In 1946, a biophysics laboratory was established at King's College, London, with physicist John Randall in charge. The idea was to hire physicists like Maurice Wilkins to work on problems in biology.

Rosalind Franklin, as a trained crystallographer, was a controversial figure. In *The Double Helix*, Watson wrote, "Maurice Wilkins could not take his mind off his assistant, Rosalind Franklin... The moment she arrived at his laboratory they began to upset each other." Rosy, as she is referred in most of Watson's book, did not consider herself to be Maurice's assistant. It appears that she was hired to conduct parallel research with Maurice, but because of a misunderstanding when she arrived at King's College and Maurice was away on vacation, she understood that the research on the structure of DNA was hers and not Wilkins's. Maurice was a beginner in x-ray diffraction work and was hoping that Rosy would help him speed up his research. But Rosy claimed that she had been given DNA for her own problem and insisted that Maurice should not take any more photographs of DNA.

Rosalind Elsie Franklin was born in London, England, on July 25, 1920. She was the daughter of a comfortable, educated, banking family. Watson described her as such: "she would not emphasize her feminine qualities. She wore no make-up and had no interest in feminine clothing. At age 31, her dresses showed all the imagination of English blue-stocking adolescents." But if we study her background, we can understand that she was a fighter that had to stand up and demand to be respected as serious scientist. In school, Rosalind excelled at science and attended one of the few girls' school in London that taught physics and chemistry. At fifteen, she decided to become a scientist. But her father was against higher education for women and wanted her to be a social worker. For a time, she relented and graduated in 1941 from Newnham College, Cambridge. In 1942, she went to work for the British Coal Utilization Research Association, making fundamental studies on carbon and graphite microstructures. This work was the basis for her doctorate in physical chemistry from Cambridge University in 1945. She spent three years (1947–1950) in Paris at the Laboratoire Central des Services Chimiques de L'Etat where she learned x-ray diffraction techniques. In 1951, she returned to England as a research associate in John Randall's biophysics laboratory at King's College. When Randall gave Franklin responsibility for DNA, nobody had worked on it for months. When Wilkins returned from his vacation, he misunderstood Franklin's role and "behaved as though she was a technical assistant" when, in fact, both scientists were peers. Maurice finally acknowledged his mistake but could not overcome it. In those days, women in British academia were not treated as equals. Only males were allowed in the university dining rooms. After hours, colleagues went to men-only pubs. Watson acknowledged that the scientific world still regarded women scientists as "mere diversions from serious thinking."

Erwin Chargaff, an Austrian American biochemist, announced in 1950 his findings from his research on DNA. He found the composition of DNA to be constant within a species but to differ widely between species. His conclusion was that there must be as many different types of DNA as there are different species. But some very important consistencies emerged. First, the number of purine bases (adenine and guanine) was always equal to the number of pyrimidine bases (cytosine and thymine). Second, the number of adenine bases is equal to the number of thymine bases and the number of guanine bases equals the number of cytosine bases. These Chargaff principles were of crucial importance in constructing the Watson-Crick model of DNA. Watson made fun of himself in *The Double Helix*, writing about a meeting between him and Chargaff:

> Chargaff, one of the world's experts on DNA was not amused by 'dark horses trying to win the race' to solve the DNA structure by model building. Only when John [Kendrew] assured him that I was not a typical American did he realize he was about to listen to a nut. Seeing me quickly reinforced his intuition. Immediately he derided my hair and accent, for since I came from Chicago I had right to act otherwise. Blandly telling him that I kept my hair long to avoid confusion with American Air Force personnel proved my mental instability.

Watson and Crick developed a model of the DNA molecule based on Maurice Wilkins's and Rosalind Franklin's x-ray pictures where "three chains twisted about each other in a way that gave rise to a crystallographic repeat every 28 Angstroms [an angstrom is a unit of length equal to one ten-billionth of a meter] along the helical axis." They invited Maurice and Rosalind to see their model. Francis demonstrated how Bessel functions (mathematical equations) gave neat answers. But Maurice and Rosalind did not share the enthusiasm for the equations. Rosalind "did not give a hoot" about the helical theory and displayed increasing irritation as Francis kept talking. In her mind, there was not a shred of evidence that DNA was helical. She became aggressive when Francis and James explained their theory that magnesium (Mg^{++}) ions held together the phosphate groups of their three chain models. She argued that "the Mg^{++} ions would be surrounded by tight shells of water molecules and so was unlikely to be the kingpins of a tight structure." James admitted that his recollection of the water content of Rosalind's DNA samples could not be right. "The awkward truth became apparent that the correct DNA model must contain at least 10 times more water than was found in our model." The meeting with Maurice and Rosalind was a fiasco. Sir Lawrence Bragg was angry that Francis Crick had stirred up a tempest with King's College. Maurice's boss complained to Sir Lawrence about Crick and the American duplicating King's work in DNA. Sir Lawrence ordered Crick to stop work on DNA. He wanted Crick to concentrate in his thesis task of investigating the ways hemoglobin crystals shrink when they are placed in salt solutions of different density. Sir Lawrence hoped that in a year to eighteen months, Crick would finish his thesis, earn his PhD, and get a job far away from Cavendish.

James and Francis did not appeal the verdict. They refrained from publicly questioning Bragg's decision. James and Francis realized that their three-chain model was flawed. It appeared that "any model placing the sugar-phosphate backbone in the center of a helix forced atoms closer together than the laws of chemistry allowed." They needed to start again.

For a while, Watson could not concentrate on DNA because he was preoccupied with sex—the mating habits of bacteria. None of his friends could guess that bacteria had sex lives. Since they had been prohibited by Sir Lawrence from working on DNA, Watson and Crick had been trying to continue research on DNA indirectly and surreptitiously by researching tobacco mosaic virus RNA (ribonucleic acid, a nucleic acid present in all living cells). But Watson and Crick were closed out from experimental data (Rosalind was more uncooperative than ever with Maurice). James went back to his thoughts about sex (of bacteria).

In January 1953, Linus Pauling wrote a paper on the structure of DNA. Two copies of the manuscript were sent to Sir Lawrence Bragg and another to his son, Peter Pauling. Bragg tried to prevent Francis from seeing it and going on a wild goose chase. But Peter Pauling showed the manuscript to Watson. James noticed that something was not right with the locations of essential actions. He could not pinpoint the mistake until he looked at the illustrations for several minutes. Then he realized that the phosphate groups in Linus's model "were not ionized, but that each group contained a bound hydrogen atom and so had no net charge." So Pauling's nucleic acid was no acid at all. "The hydrogens were part of the hydrogen bonds that held together the three intertwined chains. Without the hydrogen atoms, the chains would immediately fly apart and the structure vanishes."

Everything that James knew about nucleic-acid chemistry showed that phosphate groups never contained bound atoms. There was no question that DNA was a moderately strong acid. There should always be positively charged ions like sodium or magnesium nearby to neutralize the negatively charged phosphate groups.

Neither James nor Francis could figure out how the brilliant Linus Pauling had committed this blunder. So James and Francis were still in the race to make the great discovery of the molecular structure of DNA. But they had to move fast since Pauling was surely going to discover his mistake soon and would be working hard to correct his model.

James felt that they had to inform the King's College team about Pauling's mistake, but instead of calling Maurice Wilkins by phone, he decided to visit in person and show Pauling's manuscript to Maurice and Rosalind.

When James arrived at King's College, Maurice was busy. So James went to Rosalind's laboratory. He explained to her where Pauling had made his mistake. James could not refrain from pointing to her the similarity between Pauling's three-chain model and the model James and Francis had shown her and Maurice fifteen months before, thinking it would amuse her. But the result had the opposite effect. She was annoyed at his mentioning of a helical structure and argued that there was not a shred of evidence to allow Linus or anybody else to postulate a helical structure of DNA. James interrupted her and asserted that any regular polymeric structure was a helix. Hardly able to control her temper, Rosalind said that "the stupidity" of James's remarks would be obvious if he would look at her x-ray evidence. Several months earlier, Maurice had explained to him the nature of Rosalind's antihelical conclusions. James told her that she was incompetent (or words that implied that) in interpreting x-ray pictures and needed to learn some theory to be able to properly interpret her pictures.

Suddenly, Rosalind came from behind the lab bench and began moving toward James. Fearing that, in her uncontrollable anger, she would strike him, James grabbed the manuscript and beat a retreat toward the door where Maurice had just appeared. With Maurice and Rosalind looking at each other, James told Maurice that his conversation with Rosalind was over and that he was about to go looking for him in the Tea Room. Rosalind then firmly closed the door behind them. After James discussed the incident with Maurice, the latter agreed that Rosalind would probably have attacked him. Some months before, she made a similar lunge toward him after an argument in his room. She had blocked the door when he tried to escape and had moved out of the way at the last moment. There were no witnesses. (I wonder that, if she had struck Maurice or James, would it have been the excuse Maurice needed to send her packing?)

After Maurice "saved" James from Rosalind's fury, he confided that with his assistants, he had been quietly duplicating Rosalind's x-ray work. He mentioned that Rosalind had evidence of a three-dimensional form of DNA. It occurred when the DNA molecules were surrounded by a large amount of water. Maurice showed James a print of what they called the B structure of DNA. James was very excited when he saw the picture. The black cross of reflection in the picture could only be caused by a helical structure. Several of the helical parameters were obvious. A few minutes of calculations would give the number of chains in the molecule.

During the train ride toward Cambridge, James drew what he remembered of the B pattern on the blank edge of his newspaper. Then he tried to decide between the two- or three-chain models. By the time he had cycled back to college, he had decided to build a two-chain model. He figured that Francis would agree because, as a physicist, "he knew that important biological objects come in pairs."

The next day, James explained to Sir Lawrence Bragg what he had learned. He had no problem convincing Bragg that they needed to work on the model of the DNA molecule before Linus Pauling could beat them to it. To James's relief, Sir Lawrence encouraged him to get on with the job of building models. James dashed to the machine shop to ask for metal models of purines and pyrimidines. While waiting for the metal models to be ready, James cut representations of bases out of cardboard. That night, he went to the theater with a group of French young women who were exchange students. The next day, he started shifting the bases in his model in and out of other pairing possibilities. Suddenly, he became aware that an adenine-thymine pair held together by two hydrogen bonds was identical in shape to a guanine-cytosine pair held together by two hydrogen bonds. The bonds seemed to form naturally. He consulted with his friend Jerry Donohue, a biochemist. Jerry did not object to his base pairs. James's morale skyrocketed, for now he suspected he and Francis had the answer to the riddle of why the number of purine residues exactly equaled the number of pyrimidine residues. James wrote in *The Double Helix*:

> Two irregular sequences of bases could be regularly packed in the outer of a helix if a purine always hydrogen-bonded to a pyrimidine. Furthermore, the hydrogen bonding requirement meant that adenine would always pair with thymine, while guanine could pair only with cytosine. Chargaff's rules then suddenly stood out as a consequence of a double-helical structure for DNA. Even more exciting, this type of double helix suggested a replication scheme more satisfactory than my briefly considered like-with-like pairing. Always pairing adenine with thymine and guanine with cytosine meant that the base sequences of the two intertwined chains were complementary to each other. Given the base sequences of one chain that of its partner was automatically determined. Conceptually, it was thus very easy to visualize how a single chain could be the template for the synthesis of a chain with the complementary sequence.

When Francis arrived, James gave him an earful of his discovery. Francis pushed the bases together in a number of different ways and verified that there was no other way to satisfy Chargaff's rules. They still did not have a complete model for the DNA molecule.

But when they went later that day into the Eagle Pub, James felt queasy when Francis started "telling everyone within earshot that we had found the secret of life." The next day, they got their metal parts from the machine shop, and James put the DNA model together with the atoms in positions that satisfied the x-ray data and the laws of stereochemistry (the branch of chemistry that deals with spatial arrangements of atoms in molecules and the effects of these arrangements on chemical and physical properties of substances). Now they were able to show that at least one specific two-chain complementary helix was stereochemically possible. Before this was clear, they were afraid that the objection could be raised that the shape of the sugar-phosphate backbone might not permit its existence. But now they knew this was not true, so the structure they devised had to exist.

When Maurice Wilkins looked at the model, he immediately liked it. There was never any resentment in him about Watson and Crick making the discovery that should have been done by him and his colleagues at King's College. Two days later, he phoned James and Francis to inform them that he and Rosalind found that their x-ray data strongly supported the double helix. They wanted to publish their results simultaneously with James and Francis's announcement of the base pairs in the journal *Nature*.

Rosalind's attitude toward Watson and Crick changed dramatically. James was amazed at Rosalind's instant acceptance of their model. He had feared that she would attack the correctness of the double helix. Although originally she denied the existence of the helical structure, her x-ray evidence led her to accept it. She could not argue against the uniqueness of the A-T and G-C pairs. She shared her x-ray pictures with Francis so he could see evidence that the sugar-phosphate backbone was on the outside of the molecule. James and Francis realized that her attitude toward Maurice and them was caused by her desire to have her first-rate crystallographic ability given formal recognition.

Maurice and Rosalind peer-reviewed a draft of James and Francis's paper. Maurice and Rosalind's papers covered roughly the same areas and interpreted their results in terms of the base pairs. James's sister Elizabeth typed the final version since the Cavendish typist was not available. She enthusiastically accepted the job after being told that she would be participating "in perhaps the most famous event in biology since Darwin's book." The article was nine hundred words long. It began "we wish to suggest a structure for the salt of deoxyribose nucleic acid (DNA). This structure has novel features which are of considerable biological interest." On Wednesday, April 2, 1953, the manuscript went off to the editors of *Nature* with a strong covering letter by Sir Lawrence. In 1962, James Watson, Francis Crick, and Maurice Wilkins shared the Nobel Prize. Regretfully, Rosalind Franklin died at age thirty-seven of ovarian cancer. Her x-ray work at King's College is considered as superb. In her last years, she frequently consulted with Francis. After learning that she was terminally ill, she never complained and continued to work until a few weeks before her death. The Nobel Prize is not awarded posthumously. If she had lived, maybe it would have been her who shared the Nobel Prize with Watson and Crick.

Rachel Carson
Mother of the Environmental Movement

In 2001, I became an instructor of environmental science and ethics at the University of Phoenix. One of the references I was issued was *The Age of Environmentalism* by J. E. de Steiguer. The cover had a photo of Rachel Carson leaning against a tree. One of the first articles was "Rachel Carson's Silent Spring," which summarized the life of this remarkable woman and scientist. Intrigued, I read *Silent Spring*, the 1994 edition with an introduction by then vice president Al Gore. Years later, when I decided to write a book about scientists, I read the excellent biography by Linda Lear, *Rachel Carson: Witness for Nature*. I had to include a chapter about Rachel Carson as one of the most influential scientists of the twentieth century.

Rachel Louise Carson grew up in Springdale, Pennsylvania, a rural river town. Her mother taught her the love of nature. In 1925, she entered the Pennsylvania College for Women (PCW) as an English major, planning to become a writer. But midway through her studies, thanks to the influence of one of her teachers and mentor, Ms. Mary Scott Skinker, professor of biology at PCW, Rachel changed her major to biology. Carson's biographer, Linda Lear, wrote that Ms. Skinker "changed Rachel Carson's life."

Rachel graduated magna cum laude with a bachelors of arts degree in biology from PCW in 1929. She obtained a scholarship to study for a master's degree in zoology at John Hopkins University in Baltimore. But during the summer of 1929, Rachel was blessed with the opportunity to study during summer at the Woods Hole Martine Biological Laboratory in Massachusetts. At Woods Hole, she saw the sea for the first time in her life. The Marine Biology Laboratory (MBL) was part of the US Fish Commission. The MBL was founded in1888 as an educational center for marine biological study. Women were welcomed as students and teachers from the beginning. There was minimum hierarchy, so students and beginning investigators could work in the same laboratory along with distinguished professors and Nobel laureates. The MBL was a biologist's club that allowed scientists to relax, free from university obligations and distractions. Rachel was enchanted by Woods Hole. The inspiration for her books, especially *The Sea Around Us*, belongs to this first summer at Woods Hole. There was an excellent library with a wide selection of scientific journals from around the world and rare and new books. Rachel was one of seventy-one beginning investigators, including thirty-one women. Rachel finished her six weeks at Woods Hole, feeling more self-assured of her potential to become a zoologist with growing interest in marine biology. Rachel's goal was to complete her master's degree in zoology in the next two years at John Hopkins University.

Rachel graduated with a master of arts degree from John Hopkins University in June 1932 but with no prospect of full-time employment. She had a part-time job at the Dental and Pharmacy School at the University of Maryland. But she was not making enough money to pay for her studies for a doctor's degree and had to drop out of John Hopkins by 1934. Although her teaching ability was rated highly by her John Hopkins professors, there were few teaching positions available in 1935. The opportunities for Rachel—without a PhD at the beginning of the Great Depression—to find a teaching or research position with a university were slim.

Rachel turned to writing as a potential source of income. She sent poems and short stories she had written in college to the *Saturday Evening Post*, *Collier's*, *Poetry*, and *Reader's Digest* but received only rejection slips.

Then Rachel turned to her friend and former teacher Mary Scott Skinker. Skinker had been hired as a full-time research parasitologist in the Zoological Division of the Department of Agriculture's Bureau of Animal Industry. She was a distinguished government scientist and had completed her PhD in zoology at George Washington University in 1933. Skinker encouraged Rachel to take the civil service examinations in several zoological areas. Skinker advised Rachel about the opportunities to work as a government scientist, specifically in the US Bureau of Fisheries then at the Department of Commerce. Skinker introduced Rachel to Elmer Higgins, acting director of the US Bureau of Fisheries, Division of Scientific Inquiry. The energetic Higgins would have a critical influence on Rachel's career as a scientist and writer. Rachel passed the civil service exams and was hired for a temporary position—writing radio scripts about fisheries and marine life for the Bureau of Fisheries (now the US Fish and Wildlife Service) in Washington, DC. Within a year, the position became permanent, and during the next sixteen years, she advanced from assistant aquatic biologist to editor-in-chief of the agency.

Rachel wrote not with a cold, technical style but with a beautiful literary style that has been described as "poetic." In 1941, she published her first book, *Under the Sea-Wind*. The book received raving reviews, but it was published days from December 7, 1941, the Japanese attack at Pearl Harbor. Possibly because people were distracted with World War II, the book sold poorly—only some two thousand copies were sold, to Rachel's great disappointment. In 1951, she published a second book, *The Sea Around Us*. This book was a great success, with eighty-six weeks on the best-selling list, and eventually, an Oscar-winning documentary was made based on the book. Rachel was now a famous author and financially independent. *Under the Sea-Wind* was rereleased and became a best seller. In 1952, Rachel Carson left government service and became a full-time writer. In 1955, she published a third book, *The Edge of the Sea*. All these three books were considered "exquisite literary gems," but most importantly, they were well-researched scientific documents. Rachel estimated that in the three years required to write *The Sea Around Us*, she studied over one thousand scientific manuscripts and corresponded with many experts in the field of oceanography. She was awarded several honorary doctorates, several awards, and the deepest respect of her professional colleagues. Her literary agent, Marie Rodell, whom Carson hired in 1948, was instrumental in the success of Carson's books.

In 1957, a controversy surrounding the US Department of Agriculture's fire ant eradication program became the genesis of Rachel Carson's most famous and influential book. A lawsuit had been filed in Long Island, seeking to halt aerial spraying of private lands with DDT. Carson had learned that, by 1958, the use of chlorinated hydrocarbon and organophosphate pesticides had been greatly expanded. During the spring and summer of 1957, the USDA and several state agencies had covered Pennsylvania, New York, and New England with DDT mixed with oil to combat infestations of gypsy moth, tent caterpillar, and mosquitoes. An organic gardener and naturalist, Beatrice Trum Hunter, was the most outspoken victim of that program. She was active in the activities of the Committee Against Mass Poisoning. Federal and state agencies ignored the public outcry and planned expansion of the spraying program by January 1958. The *Boston Herald* published a letter from Mrs. Hunter where she detailed the wildlife damage that was caused by the spraying in and around her property and warned of potential health hazards to humans. Olga Owens Huckins, a writer, lecturer, and former literary editor of the *Boston Post*, and her husband owned a bird sanctuary around their home in Duxbury, Massachusetts. In 1957, Huckins's property was sprayed repeatedly for mosquitoes, resulting in the death of many songbirds and their nesting places; ponds and birdbaths had been contaminated. Carson and Huckins were friends and had been corresponding since 1951 when Huckins gave *The Sea Around Us* a great review in the *Post*. Huckins sent Carson a copy of Mrs. Hunter's *Herald* letter. Carson had been interested in the potentially harmful effects of pesticides to the environment and Huckins's letter increased her interest.

After unsuccessful attempts to interest other scholars to write a book on the subject, Carson decided to take the challenge herself. Researching the book was a daunting task. Carson had to correspond with numerous experts to request documents that had not yet been published. Mountains of scientific documents had to be researched. Shortly after starting the project, Ms. Carson's mother died, which was a blow to Carson since she and her mother lived together and were very close (Rachel never married). Carson was also raising her six-year-old nephew, Roger Christie, following the death of his mother, who was Carson's niece. Then Carson suffered a long string of illnesses, including arthritis, an ulcer, a staphylococcus infection, and finally, breast cancer, which required radiation therapy. She was aware that she only had a few years to live. She continued the research and writing for five grueling years. For most of those years, Carson did not know what she would title the book. Paul Brooks, editor-in-chief of Houghton Mifflin and Marie Rodell, would review the manuscripts and make extensive editorial comments. They let Carson know when the content was too technically difficult to understand. *Silent Spring* primarily criticized the indiscriminate spraying of agricultural insecticides and, to a lesser extent, herbicides and fungicides. Carson argued that the urge to apply over five hundred new synthetic chemicals since World War II was done without fully understanding their effects on the environment and possibly on human health. Chemicals were sprayed over large forest, agricultural, and urban areas. The general public had not been provided information about potential hazards of pesticides. Government agencies and some scientists stated—often with no evidence—that no threat existed. The government-imposed tolerance levels for pesticide contamination of fruits and vegetables were adopted with little knowledge of the human body's ability to bioaccumulate pesticides.

Like her previous books, *Silent Spring* was not merely a book of scientific essays but a work of literature. The first chapter, "A Fable for Tomorrow" starts

> There was once a town in the heart of America where all life seemed to live in harmony with its surroundings. The town lay in the midst of a checkerboard of orchards where, in spring, white clouds of bloom drifted above the green fields. In autumn, oak and maple and birch set up a blaze of color that flamed and flickered across a backdrop of pines. Then foxes barked in and deer silently crossed the fields, half hidden in the mists of the fall mornings.

The third paragraph of this short chapter reads

> Then a strange blight crept over the area and everything began to change. Some evil spell had settled on the community: mysterious maladies swept the flocks of chickens; the cattle and sheep sickened and died. Everywhere was a shadow of death. The farmers spoke of much illness among their families. In the town the doctors had become more and more puzzled by new kinds of sickness appearing among their patients. There had been several sudden and unexplained deaths, not only among adults but even among children, who would be stricken suddenly while at play and die within a few hours.

The last paragraph explains

> This town does not actually exist but it might easily have a thousand counterparts in America or elsewhere in the world. . . . Yet every one of these disasters has actually happened somewhere. . . . What has already silenced the voices of spring in countless towns of America? This book is an attempt to explain.

The book offers many research findings of eye-witness accounts of effects of pesticides on the environment. Chapter 8, "And No Bird Sings," talks about the effect of bioaccumulation and biomagnification. The book *Environmental Science* by Bernard Nebel and Richard Wright defines bioaccumulation: "Each organism accumulates the contamination in its food, so it accumulates a concentration of contaminant in its body that is many times higher than that in its food." Biomagnification is a multiplying effect that occurs through a food chain. "Essentially all the contaminant accumulated by the large biomass at the bottom of the food pyramid is concentrated, through food chains, into the smaller biomass of organisms at the top of the food pyramid."

In 1954, Professor George Wallace and graduate student John Mehner were conducting a study of robin populations around

Michigan State University in the city of East Lansing. That year, DDT spraying was conducted around campus to control elm bark beetles, which carry Dutch elm disease fungus. Dead and dying robins were noticed immediately. By late 1957, young robins were almost nonexistent where there used to be hundreds. The mystery was solved by Dr. Ray Barker of the Illinois Natural History Survey. According to Dr. Barker, DDT accumulated on tree leaves that fell to the ground and decayed into the soil. The contaminated matter was ingested by earthworms that were, in turn, eaten by the robins. This was a classic example of bioaccumulation and biomagnification in the food chain. The earthworms had minute amounts of the DDT. Since the robins ate dozens of worms each day, the DDT accumulated in their bodies to deadly levels. In the chapter "Needles Havoc," Ms. Carson describes how "aldrin, one of the most dangerous of all chlorinated hydrocarbons" was used by the Michigan Department of Agriculture with the cooperation of the US Department of Agriculture for control of the Japanese beetle in 1959. Aldrin was chosen simply because it was the cheapest of the pesticides available. State officials implied that there was no potential harm to the human population. The official answer to the question "What precautions should I take?" was "For you, none." An official of the Federal Aviation Agency was quoted in the local press, stating, "The dust is harmless to humans and will not hurt plants or pets." Ms. Carson wrote, "One must assume that none of these officials had consulted the published and readily available reports of the United States Public Health Service, the Fish and Wildlife Service, and other evidence of the extremely poisonous nature of Aldrin." The Michigan pest-control laws allowed the state to spray indiscriminately without obtaining permission of individual landowners. When the aerial spraying started, the city authorities and the Federal Aviation Agency received eight hundred calls from concerned citizens. "The pellets of insecticide fell on beetles and humans alike, showers of 'harmless' poison descending on people shopping or going to work and on children out from school for the lunch hour." Within days, reports of dead or dying birds were received by the Detroit Audubon Society. The birds showed the typical symptoms of insecticide poisoning: tremors, loss of ability to fly, paralysis, and convulsions. Veterinarians also reported dogs and cats that had sickened. And there was also at least one report of human exposure and illness: "[a] prominent Detroit internist was called upon to treat four of his patients within an hour after they had been exposed while watching the planes at work. All had similar symptoms: nausea, vomiting, chills, fever, extreme fatigue and coughing."

In the community of Sheldon in Eastern Illinois in 1954, the US Department of Agriculture and the Illinois Agriculture Department began a program to eradicate the Japanese beetle. Dieldrin was the insecticide of choice. It is interesting to note that although there was plenty of funding for chemical control, the biologists of the Illinois Natural History Survey—who were tasked with measuring the damage to wildlife—were receiving extremely low funding. Despite this, the biologists were able to document almost unparalleled wildlife destruction.

Dieldrin was applied at a rate of 3 pounds per acre. Since laboratory experiments on quail had shown dieldrin to be fifty times as poisonous as DDT, the amount of poison spread over the landscape at Sheldon was the equivalent to 150 pounds of DDT per acre. The conditions were perfect to kill insect-eating birds. Various species of birds—including brown thrashers, starlings, meadowlarks, grackles, and pheasants—were virtually wiped out. Robins were "almost annihilated" according to the biologist's report.

Ground squirrels were "virtually annihilated; their bodies were found in attitudes characteristics of violent death by poisoning." Dead muskrats and rabbits were found in the fields. The fox squirrel was gone. Ninety percent of all farm cats died during the first season of spraying. Cats are extremely sensitive to insecticides. According to Rachel Carson, the death of many cats had been documented during the antimalarial program conducted by the World Health Organization in Central Java and Venezuela; in the latter, cats were reduced to the status of a rare animal. The Natural History Survey report also documented deadly effects on several flocks of sheep and a herd of beef.

In 1955, the Natural History Survey ran out of money for its research although aerial spraying continued. Although it requested money every year, it was the first item to be eliminated. It was not until 1960 that it got some money to hire one field assistant to do the job of four biologists. In the meantime, the chemical had been changed to aldrin—one hundred to three hundred times as toxic as DDT in tests on quail. By 1960, every species of wild animal known to inhabit the area had suffered losses. "Pheasant hunting, which had been good in these areas in former years, was virtually abandoned as unrewarding." Ms. Carson described the contrast between pesticide spraying in Illinois and other states with biological controls introduced in eastern states for the Japanese beetle. During the first dozen years after its entry into the United States in 1912, the beetle population increased rapidly. But by 1945, it had become a pest of only minor importance. Its decline was largely a result of the importation of parasitic insects from the Far East and the establishment of disease organisms fatal to it.

Between 1920 and 1933, scientists identified and introduced into the territory where the Japanese beetle lived, some thirty-four species of predatory insects from the Orient. The most successful was a parasitic wasp from Korea and China, *Tiphia vernalis*. The female *Tiphia* injects a paralyzing fluid into a beetle grub and attaches a single egg to the undersurface of the grub. The young wasp, hatching as a larva, feeds on the paralyzed grub and destroys it. Another more important control was a bacterial disease popularly called milky disease. It affects beetles of the family to which the Japanese beetle belongs, but it is harmless to earthworms, warm-blooded animals, and plants. The spores of the disease occur in soil; when ingested by a beetle grub, they quickly multiply in its blood, causing it to turn an abnormally white color hence the name "milky disease." The eastern areas where this program was carried out now enjoy a high degree of natural protection from the beetle. Why were these biological controls not implemented in the midwestern states instead of aerial chemical spraying? Ms. Carson was told that inoculation with milky disease was "too expensive," but how the Department of Agriculture reached the conclusion that it was too expensive was not explained. Ms. Carson wrote, "Incidents like the eastern Illinois spraying raise a question that is not only scientific but moral. The question is whether any civilization can wage relentless war on life without destroying itself, and without losing the right to be called civilized."

Rachel Carson did not ask for complete banning of all insecticide spraying. Instead, she said,

> I am not one who feels you can eliminate all spraying by any means . . . I doubt that it is possible from the practical standpoint . . . but I do think that one great trouble—and I suppose it is the fault of the American public as a whole—is this desire for the quick and easy way of doing something, without any consideration of the consequences . . . there is still a great temptation to go ahead and get the job done and let the future take care of itself.

Here is a translation: scientists, such as those in the USDA, should do a better job of studying pests and find alternative controls, preferably those that specifically target the particular pest instead of broad spectrum insecticides.

During most of the four years that took Rachel to research and write the book, Rachel Carson did not know what its title would be. In 1960, her agent, Marie Rodell—thinking that the bird chapter was so beautiful—suggested *Silent Spring* for the title of the book. Months later, Marie was able to convince Rachel of adopting *Silent Spring* as the title after she found lines from the English poet John Keats's poem "La Belle Dame sans Merci." The lines were "The sedge is withred from the lake,/And no birds sing." Rachel agreed, and the book became *Silent Spring*.

In 1960, Rachel was diagnosed as having cysts in her left breast, one of them "suspicious enough to require a radical mastectomy." It took months for Rachel to recover from the surgery. Afterward, Rachel discovered that her physician had not told her the whole truth; the "cyst" had been a malignant tumor. The physician did not refer her for additional treatment. In the 1950s, medical protocols did not require medical doctors to tell a female patient that she had a malignancy. Perhaps he did not refer her for further treatment because he thought it would make no difference in her condition. Eventually, Rachel underwent radiation treatment, which delayed the completion of her book and caused great stress to Rachel.

In January 1962, Rachel sent fifteen chapters of *Silent Spring* to William Shawn, editor of *The New Yorker* magazine. After reading the manuscript, Shawn called Rachel and told her it was "a brilliant achievement." "You have made it literature, full of beauty and loveliness and depth of feeling." He wanted to publish chapters of the book in *The New Yorker* in the spring. Rachel put her nephew, Roger, to sleep; took her dog, Jeffie, to the study; put her arms around the dog; and let the tears come, releasing the tension of four years.

The New Yorker articles caused uproar. An enormous amount of letters fell upon the Congress, the agriculture and interior departments, the Public Health Service, and the Food and Drug Administration.

The reaction from the chemical industry was swift. A major chemical producer, Velsicol, the sole manufacturer of chlordane and heptachlor, threatened to sue the publisher of the book, Houghton Mifflin Company. Velsicol's general counsel, Louis McLean, suggested that Rachel may be part of a conspiracy. He suggested that a lawsuit may follow. Velsicol also threatened *The New Yorker* against publishing the third installment. The legal counsel for *The New Yorker*, Milton Greenstein, replied to Velsicol and other companies threatening with lawsuits: "Everything in those articles has been checked and is true. Go ahead and sue." Carson's lawyer, Maurice Greenbaum, sent the same message to Velsicol. Houghton Mifflin replied to Velsicol that the book was both fair and accurate and that Carson had provided complete references for all her material. Velsicol's lawyers then threatened the staff of the National Audubon Society, which was planning to publish *Silent Spring* in their *Audubon* magazine to no avail. The magazine not only published the articles but wrote an editorial criticizing the chemical industry's threats.

The editorial staffs of both Houghton Mifflin and the National Audubon Society have to be admired for their unflinching bravery in the face of threats from lawyers of a wealthy and powerful chemical industry. Book of the Month Club offered *Silent Spring* as the October 1962 selection. Supreme Court Justice William O. Douglas wrote for Houghton and Mifflin a review comment in which he called *Silent Spring* "the most revolutionary book since

Uncle Tom's Cabin." For Book of the Month Club, he wrote, "This book is the most important chronicle of this century for the human race. The book is a call for immediate action for effective control of all merchants of poison." The club's first printing was 150,000 copies.

At about this time, President John F. Kennedy gave a press conference. A reporter asked the president if he considered asking the Department of Agriculture or the Public Health Service to investigate the dangerous long-term effects of pesticides. The president replied, "Yes, and I know that they already are. I think particularly, of course, since Miss Carson's book, but they are examining the matter." Kennedy did not mention that a special interagency panel set up by the Federal Council for Science and Technology was investigating the matter, nor did he mention that Dr. Jerome Wiesner, special science advisor for the president, had instructed the Life Sciences Panel of the president's Science Advisory Committee to do its own study of pesticides.

An exception to the favorable coverage by the press, regretfully, was an article in *Time* magazine of September 18, 1962, which accused Rachel of "frightening and arousing her readers" and of using "emotion-fanning words." It also said that *Silent Spring* was "unfair, one-sided and hysterical." Other adversaries called Rachel Carson "a communist," "a priestess of nature," and "a devotee of a mystical cult."

While the controversy over *Silent Spring* grew, Rachel's poor health forced her to distance herself from the fray. But in April 1963, she was interviewed on the CBS report "The Silent Spring of Rachel Carson." Rachel was interviewed by CBS correspondent Eric Sevareid in her wood-paneled study, sitting calmly in her office chair. She read passages from six chapters of *Silent Spring* in her calm voice. While she read, viewers saw examples of pesticide use and abuse. She appeared as a dignified, polite, and concerned scientist.

Her adversary was industrial biochemist, Dr. Robert White-Stevens of the American Cyanamid Company. He was a strong defender of pesticides and a critic of *Silent Spring*. To CBS's credit and good judgment, Rachel and Dr. White-Stevens were not interviewed sitting next to each other where Dr. White-Stevens would have constantly interrupted her as regretfully happens so frequently today in news shows. Dr. White-Stevens was interviewed separately in his laboratory in a white lab coat. Biographer Linda Lear describes him as "wild-eyed, loud voiced." In contrast, Lear wrote, "Carson appeared anything but the hysterical alarmist that her critics contended." White-Stevens said, "If man were to faithfully follow the teachings of Miss Carson, we would return to the Dark Ages, and the insects and diseases and vermin would once again inherit the earth."

One month after the CBS special, in May 1963, the United States Office of Science and Technology, published a report titled "Use of Pesticides." The report, written by a group of distinguished scientists, was an official endorsement of *Silent Spring*. An official from the Department of the Interior said Rachel was "many, many times better informed than her critics." The Office of Science and Technology report silenced Rachel's critics (for a while) and cleared her name. She appeared before committees of the United States Senate and the House of Representatives. *Silent Spring*'s popularity continued to grow, and by the end of the year, it was selling in England, France, Germany, Italy, Denmark, Sweden, Norway, Finland, and Holland.

But Rachel's health continued to deteriorate. She was weakened by cancer and arthritis; she suffered a heart attack that left her almost an invalid. She died on April 14, 1964, at age fifty-six. Part of her ashes were buried next to her mother in a cemetery in Montgomery County, Maryland. The rest were scattered along the coast near her summer home at Newagen, Maine. In her last will, she named her editor, Paul Brooks, to be guardian of her nephew, Roger, who grew up to be a recording engineer in Massachusetts.

Silent Spring was instrumental in the birth of the environmental movement in the United States and the creation of the Environmental Protection Agency in 1970. DDT was banned in the United States and in many countries around the world. Today, DDT is classified as a probable human carcinogen by the United States and international authorities. DDT is still used in some countries for control of malaria. Other persistent pesticides, like chlordane, were banned in the United States years later. The Federal Insecticide, Fungicide, and Rodenticide Act (FIFRA) authorizes the US Environmental Protection Agency (USEPA) to review and register agrochemicals for specified uses and grants USEPA the authority to suspend or cancel registrations if it is shown that continued use would pose unreasonable risk to human health or the environment. Pest applicators using pesticides regulated by USEPA must be licensed and trained to use those chemicals safely.

Integrated pest management (IPM) is a technique to minimize the use of synthetic organic pesticides without endangering crops. Crops are rotated, and multiple crops—instead of a single crop—are planted. Spraying is not done during the growing season to encourage natural enemies of pests to flourish. The goal is to maintain crop damage by insects below the economic threshold through monitoring the insect population by means of traps and specially trained field scouts. Limited spraying is done to reduce the numbers of insects below the economic threshold. This technique has been used successfully in Indonesia in cooperation between the Food and Agricultural Organization (FAO) of the United Nations and the government of Indonesia. Rice farmers saved considerable money by reducing purchases of expensive pesticides; fish are thriving again in the rice paddies, and yields of rice have increased.

However, there are still powerful politicians and other persons in the United States that continue to attack Rachel Carson and *Silent Spring*. Groups of congressmen have voted, unsuccessfully, to repeal environmental laws. In 1971, seven years after Rachel Carson died, Dr. Robert White-Stevens, then a professor at Rutgers University in New Jersey, gave an address at the Fifty-Second Annual Meeting of the American Farm Bureau Federation entitled "A Perspective on Pesticides." Among other arguments, Dr. White-Stevens said, "Unreasonable public fear of scientific technology in general, and of agricultural chemicals specifically, gives rise to various criticisms, but there is no point in banning pesticides until there is an equally efficient way found to do their job."

In May 2007, Senator Tom Coburn (R-Oklahoma) blocked a bill that would have named a post office in Springdale, Pennsylvania, in Carson's honor. He said that Carson had "stigmatized perfectly good chemicals and that by working to ban pesticides Carson is in fact responsible for the death of millions of Africans, particularly Ugandans, from malaria." He referred to *Silent Spring* as "junk science."

Even in the United States, there are still thousands of farmworkers exposed to hazardous levels of pesticides. The Hill's Congress Blog published an article on July 15, 2013, entitled "Protecting Farmworkers from Toxic Pesticide Exposure." The article states, "Pesticide exposure causes farmworkers to suffer more chemical-related injuries and illnesses than any other work force nation-wide."

But despite the horrible attacks of industry and politicians, environmentalists and environmental scientists continue their fight, undaunted. As Rachel Carson would say, the goal is not to ban pesticides but to learn to use them safely.

Norman Borlaug
and His Army of Hunger Fighters

Obviously, I am personally honored beyond all dreams by my election. But the obligations imposed by the honor are far greater than the honor itself, both as concerns me personally and also the army of hunger fighters which I voluntarily enlisted a quarter of a century ago for a lifetime term.

—Norman Borlaug's acceptance speech,
on the occasion of the award of the
Nobel Peace Prize in Oslo, December 10, 1970.

My father was an agronomist in Puerto Rico. He graduated from the College of Agriculture and Mechanical Arts of the University of Puerto Rico in 1943. A few years earlier, J. George (Dutch) Harrar, who would eventually become Norman Borlaug's superior in Mexico while working for the Rockefeller Foundation, had spent four years in Puerto Rico teaching and working on plant diseases and botany. In 1976, I graduated from the same campus but with a degree in chemical engineering. If I had known about Norman Borlaug at the time, maybe I would have become an agronomist. In 1966, my father took my mother, my brother, my sister, and me with him to Costa Rica where he worked as professor at the Inter-American Institute of Agricultural Science (IICA) of the Organization of American States until 1968. I feel that this experience gives me some insight into what Dr. Borlaug and his family experienced in Mexico.

I learned about Dr. Norman Borlaug in 2007 while I was living in Dallas, Texas. I read about his award of the Congressional Gold Medal. I found out that a book had just been published—*The Man Who Fed the World: Nobel Peace Prize Laureate Norm Borlaug and His Battle to End World Hunger* by Leon Hesser. I asked my wife to buy me the book for my birthday. I learned that Dr. Borlaug lived only fifteen miles from my house, and twice, I drove by his house hoping to catch him working in his yard so I could ask him for his autograph. But, alas, he was not outside and I could not muster the courage to knock on his door. Perhaps he would have been teaching at Texas A&M or visiting the International Maize and Wheat Improvement Center (CIMMYT) in Mexico or perhaps even working in Africa with the Sasakawa Africa Association. He was still very active at the age of ninety-four. He died of cancer on September 12, 2009, so now I'll never be able to have him autograph my copy of his biography. But at least I could summarize his life in one chapter of my book. Leon Hesser's book was my main source for this chapter.

Norman Borlaug was born in Saude, Iowa, on the farm of his grandfather and, since the age of seven, worked on the farm. He attended a one-room schoolhouse. In high school, he excelled in sports, especially wrestling. Years later, he would be inducted into the National Wrestling Hall of Fame in Stillwater, Oklahoma. Despite the economic hardships of the Great Depression, his grandfather encouraged him to leave the farm and pursue higher education. A federal program, the National Youth Administration, made it possible for him to attend the University of Minnesota where he met Margaret Gibson whom he would eventually marry.

He failed the entrance examination because of the poor schools he had to attend in his youth and had to enroll in the General College to broaden his education. Eventually, he joined the forestry program of the University's College of Agriculture. At the end of his bachelor's degree in 1937, he got a job offer as a full-time assistant ranger in the Idaho National Forest. He accepted and asked Margaret to marry him. They were married on September 27, 1937. But before Norman finished his bachelor's degree, he was notified that because of budget cuts, his position with the Idaho National Forest could not be funded. Margaret convinced him to do postgraduate studies. Norman had attended a lecture by the distinguished scientist Dr. E. C. Stakman, head of the Department of Plant Pathology and had told Margaret "One day I would like to go back and study under that man if it is ever possible." He now knocked on Dr. Stakman and told him he would like to study for a master's degree in forest pathology. Dr. Stakman said, "I'll tell you what I think. I think most forest pathologists starve to death. You should go into plant pathology—that will give you more flexibility."

Norman enrolled in a master's program on plant pathology and Dr. Stakman helped him get a paid assistantship in the Department of Plant Pathology with a small salary, and his tuition was waived. He obtained his master's degree in 1940 and was designated an instructor and given a two-bedroom apartment at the university while he pursued his doctorate degree. In October 1941, while writing his doctoral dissertation, he received an offer from E. I. du Pont de Nemours & Company of $2,800 per year as head of a biochemical laboratory to develop agricultural chemicals at Wilmington, Delaware. He accepted the offer, finished his doctorate, and he and Margaret headed for a secure future. When the United States entered World War II, Norman tried to enlist in the army but was refused for military service because his job was considered essential to the war effort. DuPont switched the focus of his laboratory from agricultural chemicals to new developments in camouflage, disinfectants, malaria prevention, and insulation for electronic devices. The most significant achievement of his laboratory was the development of a waterproof adhesive for sealing seaborne supply packages. The Academy of Achievement documented that "with the Marines pinned down in Guadalcanal, Borlaug and his team developed the new adhesive in a manner of weeks, enabling the Marines to hold out until the Japanese were driven from the island."

Mexico

During this time, Dr. Stackman had been recruited by the Rockefeller Foundation to help Mexico overcome the devastation of its agriculture by a parasitic fungus called stem rust. Let's go back and discuss the background for this initiative. In November 1940, Franklin Delano Roosevelt was reelected president of the United States. His vice president–elect was former secretary of agriculture Henry A. Wallace. Henry Wallace had studied agriculture at Iowa State College. After graduating in 1910, he started experimenting with hybrid corn, and by 1923, he had developed the first commercially viable strain of hybrid corn. In 1926, he founded the Hi-Bred Corn Co. (now Pioneer Hi-Bred International). He revolutionized corn production, first in Iowa and then through the Midwest. The percent of hybrid corn planted in the United States grew from less than 1 percent in 1933 to 78 percent by 1943, and the average corn yield grew from twenty-four bushels per acre to thirty-one bushels per acre by 1941. Following his election as vice president, Henry Wallace decided to take a trip through Latin America to improve his fluency in Spanish. But Franklin Roosevelt convinced him of going to Mexico instead to serve as ambassador extraordinary during the inauguration of General Avila Camacho as president of Mexico.

A truly extraordinary man, Wallace drove his own car with his wife, Ilo, to Mexico City without any security so he could stop on the way and chat, in Spanish, with Mexican farmers and their families and talk about agriculture and observe their fields. Later, accompanied by the Mexican minister of agriculture, he conducted a personal inspection tour of Mexican agriculture and was appalled to find out that per capita food production was falling despite agrarian reform. The outgoing president of Mexico, Lazaro Cardenas, had broken up the giant estates of the old ruling class and divided the land into small holdings. But the small Mexican farmers lacked the know-how, equipment, and capital to get the most yields from their farms. Fertilizer was too expensive for them. The best farms produced only twenty bushels of corn to the acre; most farms produced only ten bushels per acre. Wheat was devastated by rust. When Wallace returned to the United States, he persuaded the Rockefeller Foundation to help the Mexican government to increase the production of corn and wheat. The Rockefeller Foundation had been in Mexico for two decades as part of a cooperative public health program.

The Rockefeller Foundation was formed in 1913. It has been a trailblazer in the field of public health—with campaigns against diseases and epidemics, supporting the development of public health schools all over the world. Scientists, economists, scholar, and grassroots leaders supported by the foundation have helped solve some of the world's most challenging problems. And on February 3, 1941, the foundation president, Raymond D. Fosdick, met with Vice President Wallace to discuss the foundation's assistance to México. Wallace suggested that the foundation change its focus from public health to food production. The Mexican minister of agriculture, Marte R. Gomez, asked the foundation to help increase production of corn.

The Rockefeller Foundation took on the challenge. Since the foundation's basic policy was to know the facts before going into action, they decided to send a team of scientists on a survey mission to Mexico. They hired E. C. Stakman who was a professor at the University of Minnesota, who was internationally recognized for his work on plant pathology, and who spoke six languages, including Spanish. Two other members of the team with international reputations included Richard Bradfield, who was professor of soil science at Cornell, and Paul C. Magelsdorf, professor of plant pathology and economic botany at Harvard. Several Mexican scientists made up the rest of the group.

After studying the situation in several of Mexico's states, Stakman came up with a plan of action: the foundation should field a team of four dedicated and competent scientists. Their mission would be to cooperate with the government of Mexico to develop improved plant varieties, specifically for corn and wheat and some attention to beans and some other crops. The Rockefeller Foundation's other agricultural program was in China in 1935, but it had been limited to providing funds. In Mexico, it would provide assistance to direct and operate the program, as well as to provide funds.

In 1943, the Mexican Government–Rockefeller Foundation Cooperative Agricultural Program was born. It would be America's first foreign agricultural assistance program.

Dr. Stakman recommended J. "Dutch" Harrar who had earned a PhD as one of Stakman's students at the University of

Minnesota. Prior to going to the University of Minnesota, Harrar, after earning a master's degree from Iowa State, had spent four years at the University of Puerto Rico teaching and working on plant diseases and botany. He spoke fluent Spanish. After earning his PhD, Harrar had taught for five years at Virginia Polytechnic Institute and had been recently named head of the Department of Pathology at Washington State University. They hired geneticist corn-breeder Dr. Edwin Wellhausen and Dr. William Colwell, an agronomist soil scientist.

Now Stakman and Harrar went out to hire Borlaug. Harrar told Borlaug that the team he was putting together was going to conquer hunger in Mexico. "I would like for you to work on diseases of all crops in or program with special emphasis on wheat." Borlaug asked advice from Stakman who told him "Norman, you are the best man for the job . . . But if I can encourage you, Norman, I'll say this: it would be a worthwhile thing to do, to put bread into those hungry bellies in Mexico."

Then Norman asked advice from the most important person in his life—his wife, Margaret. He asked, why should he give up a good job with DuPont to "put bread into those hungry bellies in Mexico?" She answered, "But Norman, you know you've always felt a need to do something to help hungry people." He was worried about how she would cope with raising their daughter Jeanie and the baby that was due in a couple of months. Margaret assured him that he did not have to worry about her. "Now you go. I'll join you when you are settled."

And off Norman Bourlaug went to meet his destiny in Mexico. What awaited him was no paradise. He rode from Laredo, Texas, to Mexico City with Wellhausen and his wife, Vivian. Wellhausen explained to Borlaug what it was like to work in Mexico. There were no modern experimental field stations and only a few trained Mexican agronomists. The 800 acres of land surrounding the agricultural school in Chapingo, twenty miles northeast of Mexico City, was mostly unused and overgrown with weeds. Harrar had been given 150 acres there to set up an experimental corn and wheat-breeding station, but there was no equipment. The Rockefeller Foundation could not help with tractors, trucks, or major farm equipment because these were wartime priorities.

Gasoline and spare tires were nearly impossible to obtain. The only building was an adobe shed with a tar-paper roof. The minister of agriculture, Dr. Marte R. Gomez, was eager to cooperate, but the bureaucracy moved slowly.

At the Office of Special Studies, Harrar explained to Borlaug the background of the Mexican 1910–1918 revolution. After the revolution, fifty million hectares of land had been transferred from large landowners to small-scale farmers (campesinos). The farmers lacked the knowledge, skills, and money needed to operate their small farms productively. After thirty years, the reform had failed to end poverty, ignorance, and hunger. The Rockefeller Foundation was committed to foment a bloodless revolution and double food production through transformation of technology. Norman thought, *What kind of future is there for me in this strange country?*

At the experimental station at Chapingo, Borlaug and Harrar concentrated on wheat, Wellhausen on corn, and Coldwell on soil-fertility tests. He and Wellhausen visited the great central agricultural region, the Bajio, to try to recruit farmers to allow them to plant test plots of corn and wheat on their lands. But they found hopelessness. Most farmers could not read or write. The land was devoid of nutrients, and fertilizer was mostly unknown.

On November 9, 1944, Margaret called Norman and informed him that their baby Scott was born with a spina bifida (an incomplete closure of the spinal column), a rare, fatal condition. The baby was not expected to live long. Norman spent a week with Margaret, Jeanie, and baby Scott. The doctor urged Margaret to go join Norman in Mexico. "There is nothing medically that can be done for Scotty; It's just a matter of time. It would be best if you left him here in the hospital and joined your husband." Margaret and Jeanie travelled by train to Mexico City and joined Norman. A few months later, they received word that little Scott had died peacefully.

In March 1945, Harrar told Borlaug that he had too much work at the Office of Special Studies and put Borlaug in charge of the Cooperative Wheat Research and Production Program.

Wheat is an ancient grain that has been consumed for over twelve thousand years. Wheat is the dietary staple of many regions of the world. Wheat was not native to the western hemisphere and was introduced here in the late fifteenth century when Columbus came to the New World.

Borlaug's job was to do whatever was necessary to increase Mexico's wheat production. It was tough, tedious, and complex work involving experimental plot development, planting, recruiting helpers, and training young scientists and technicians. He and his team planted demonstration plots on farmer's fields using seeds of better varieties, fertilizer, improved irrigation practices, and weed control. They were to train local scientists. He and his team were to be neither consultants nor advisors but working scientists getting their hands and boots dirty. One of Norman's Mexican colleagues argued that in Mexico, scientists did not work in the fields but they would draw up plans, give them to the foreman, and let him and the peons do the job. Norman lost his temper, something that seldom happened, raised his voice, and told the Mexican scientist that farmers would have no respect for them if they did not know how to do the job themselves; if the peons gave false information, they could not know. They needed to master their own efforts, or the project would go nowhere. And from then on, the Mexican scientists worked in the field side by side with Borlaug.

Then Borlaug and his team attacked the great enemy of wheat harvests: stem rust. Between 1939 and 1942, stem rust had destroyed half of Mexico's wheat harvest. The most important wheat production region, Sonora, had suffered the most damage. Borlaug's challenge was to develop varieties of wheat resistant to stem rust. He had to crossbreed hundreds of lines, hoping to find at least one line that would be resistant to stem rust. Most plant breeders made only a few dozen crosses in a year, selected the best plants, and planted them the next year; the process typically took six or seven years. In order to speed up the process, Borlaug collected thousands of varieties of wheat from around the world, and he and his scientists began to plant and crossbreed them. Crossbreeding by hand is a delicate, tedious operation. It required an immense amount of work. Borlaug worked from sunrise to sunset, often sleeping at the field station in a sleeping bag and cooking meals over an open campfire. But eventually, his hard work paid off. The rust-resistant varieties of wheat he developed produced yields 20 to 40 percent higher than the original varieties.

Leon Hesser wrote in *The Man Who Fed the World*: "Borlaug never wasted time searching for the perfect variety, but after adequate testing released for commercial use the best available at that point in time." This is *pragmatism*. Leon Hesser further quoted Borlaug saying "Perfection is a butterfly the academics chase and never catch. If we go on looking for the ideal wheat for Mexico, your countrymen will go on being hungry for a long time."

After a visit to an abandoned experimental station near Ciudad Obregon in the Yaqui Valley about two thousand kilometers North West of Mexico City, Norman conceived the idea of shuttle breeding. This concept consisted of planting wheat seeds from the Yaqui Valley at the highlands of Chapingo and Toluca near Mexico City during summer then harvesting the seeds and planting them at the Yaqui Valley during winter (because of the differences in altitude and temperature, the planning seasons were different at Toluca and the Yaqui in different times of the year). He could grow two generations of wheat per year instead of one. This would cut the breeding time in half.

Then there was a clash between Norman Borlaug and George Harrar that could have killed the Green Revolution before it was born. In a subsequent meeting with the Rockefeller Foundation agricultural advisory committee, Borlaug's plan met resistance. Borlaug demanded authority to delegate a good share of effort of the wheat program to the Sonora region and to be allowed to do it in the way he thought best. Harrar exclaimed, "Goddammit, Norm, this scheme of yours has been considered twice, at your insistence, and voted down twice. Why can't you accept that?" Borlaug replied, "If this is a firm decision, I also make a firm decision. You will have to find someone else to conform to your rules." Dr. Stakman, who was present, asked Norman not to "go jumping the gun," but Norman said, "As of now I resign. You'll have it in writing first thing tomorrow," and he left the room.

Early the next morning, when Norman arrived at his office, he found Dr. Stakman waiting for him. After Stakman rebuked him for flying off the handle the previous day, he was able to convince Norman to wait until later that day to write his resignation. And then, a miracle happened. That day, Harrar received a letter from a prominent farmer from Sonora expressing admiration for

Norman Borlaug. The farmer wrote, "For the first time, Dr. Harrar, I have seen a man come here from the Rockefeller Foundation or any other organization to help the farmer. Perhaps it is the first time in the history of Mexico that any scientist tried to help our farmers—I don't know that. The results are already evident in my own land with this new, wonderful wheat. I thank you, and I thank Dr. Borlaug . . . I want to say that what is happening here with Dr. Borlaug will have a tremendous effect within a short time." Between Stakman's intervention with Harrar and the farmer's letter, shuttle breeding was saved. When Borlaug came back to the office, Stakman and Harrar were waiting. Harrar shook hands with Borlaug and told him that the matter had been reconsidered. Now, Borlaug had Harrar's approval for the shuttle-breeding program. That fall, Norman flew to Ciudad Obregon with two bags of seed of the newest varieties from the breeding program and thousands of other promising seeds.

The shuttle-breeding program succeeded beyond Norman's wildest expectations. Not only did they advance the generations of plants twice as fast, but by growing the plants at different latitudes and altitudes, the plants were exposed to different soils, climates, and diseases. The result was plants that were adapted to a wide range of conditions. Shuttle breeding was adopted worldwide.

Then Norman attacked another problem with Mexican wheat. Mexican varieties were slender and tall. The problem was that they were not able to use large application of fertilizer to increase yields. When fertilized, they grew tall, but with wind and the increased weight of grain, they got heavy and fell to the ground before ripening; a lot of wheat was lost. Norman began a search of different wheat varieties from around the world to find one with short stronger stems. He grew over twenty thousand varieties without success. But then he learned that in late 1952, Dr. Orville Vogel—a wheat breeder in the US Department of Agriculture, stationed at Washington State University—had obtained some success with crossing a Japanese dwarf winter-habit wheat with the tall US winter wheat. In 1953, Borlaug obtained a few seeds from Vogel's most successful lines and started crossing them with the most promising Mexican varieties. He developed a new type of wheat, short and stiff strawed. This wheat thrust up more stems from the base of the plant and had more grains per head. After crossing and recrossing, he gave rise to a group of what would be called dwarf Mexican wheat varieties. This had the potential from increasing the yield under ideal conditions—from 4,500 kilos per hectare to 9,000 kilos per hectare. A former governor, Don Rodolfo Calles, saw Norman's success with wheat. He got land for a new station in Sonora. According to Norman, "Don Rodolfo then organized farmer's groups, protected them from bureaucrats and changed everything for the better."

By 1956, Mexico was self-sufficient in wheat production by growing more than forty new, high-yielding, and rust-resistant varieties developed by Dr. Borlaug.

India

In 1967, William and Paul Paddock published their book *Famine 1975! America's Decision: Who Will Survive?* They believed that famine in a vast scale was inevitable, and efforts to prevent famine should be restricted to areas where there was some hope of success. India was written off as hopeless.

In 1968, Paul Ehrlich (biologist and environmentalist) published the book *The Population Bomb* about the need for population control. He predicted that food production could not possibly keep up with increases in human population. India and Pakistan were among the highest contributors to the world population explosion and had to import vast amounts of American wheat under the Food for Peace program to barely meet their food needs. By this time, Borlaug's high-yielding Mexican wheat began to appear in the Asian subcontinent. Borlaug arranged for the Rockefeller Foundation to hire Dr. Glenn Anderson, wheat expert and gung ho leader from the Canadian Department of Agriculture, and send him to India. He also got his highly esteemed Dr. Ignacio Narvaez from Mexico to be sent to Pakistan under a Ford Foundation grant.

Borlaug had warned his international students in Mexico not to try to change the way wheat was grown in their countries too quickly. In later visits to Pakistan and Egypt, his former students confirmed this problem when they showed Borlaug excellent patches of Mexican wheat they had grown in their "private" plots using the technology and husbandry that Borlaug taught them. In contrast, the wheat grown in other parts of their country's agricultural experimental stations was not doing so well. The conventional wisdom was that agricultural progress in developing countries would be slow. So Borlaug came up with what he called the kick-off approach to overcome the conventional wisdom and obtain rapid results. This approach was founded on manipulating three factors: technical, psychological, and economic. The field trials had proven that Mexican wheat could grow well in Asia and the Middle East. The challenges were the psychological and economic factors.

In 1966, a drought in India caused mixed results in test half-acre plots in thousands of farms. But many were good and several were excellent. In some areas, the results were much better than anything ever achieved before. Then the minister of food and agriculture, Subramaniam, "made a courageous and historic decision. Against the advice of several of his senior scientists, he decided to import eighteen thousand tons of the short-strawed, high-yielding Lerma Rojo 64 seed from Mexico." In the fall of 1966, 240,000 hectares were planted with Mexican varieties of wheat. But before the plantings, there was a great controversy with economists over the use of fertilizer. On one side, economists from the Ministry of Agriculture, the Planning Commission, and the Rockefeller Foundation with Norman Borlaug and Glenn Anderson on the other side argued heatedly. The economists wanted to cut back fertilizer application to one-third per hectare so that fertilizer could be spread over three times more area. But Borlaug and Anderson argued that this cutback was premature. The debate turned emotional and heated, but thanks to the diplomacy of Dr. Ralph Cummings, who headed the Rockefeller Foundation team in India, all sides calmed down. A heavy rate of fertilizer was applied to the 240,000 hectares, and the dramatic results gave victory to Borlaug and Anderson.

Then India's prime minister, Indira Ghandi, planted some Mexican wheat in front of her house, which developed beautifully and fulfilled its psychological purpose. By 1968, there was euphoria in the wheat-growing region of India. Farmers, scientists, professors, and even bureaucrats were excited about Mexican wheat.

At a luncheon at a tractor factory where members of the New Delhi press were present, Borlaug said, "I wish I were now a member of India's Congress; I would stand up out-of-order every few minutes and shout in a loud voice: what India needs now is fertilizer, fertilizer, fertilizer, credit, credit, credit, and fair prices, fair prices, fair prices!"

Before leaving India, Borlaug had a stormy meeting with Deputy Prime Minister Ashoka Metha about the need for India to greatly increase availability of fertilizer to farmers by increasing imports of fertilizer and building fertilizer-manufacturing plants in India, as well as providing credits to farmers to purchase fertilizer. Minister Metha argued that India could not afford any of this. But only two weeks after Norman returned to Mexico, he received newspaper clippings from the Rockefeller Foundation in India about the drastic change in policy on fertilizer imports and the expansion of domestic fertilizer production. Eventually, this resulted in dramatic increases in food production.

In *The Population Bomb* in 1968, Paul Ehrlich wrote that it was "a fantasy" that India would ever feed itself. By 1974, India was self-sufficient in the production of all cereals.

Pakistan

Pakistan in the mid-1960s was also struggling to feed its population. It relied on food aid under the Food for Peace program. But they needed a permanent solution to their food problem.

In late 1965, agricultural economist Leon Hesser, who—years later—would write *The Man Who Fed the World*, was recruited by the US Agency for International Development to work as assistant to the director of the USAID technical assistant program for agriculture in Pakistan. Soon after arriving in Pakistan, Hesser was promoted to chief of the agriculture division. But to really expand their program, they needed a catalyst. And then entered Norman Borlaug. He briefed Hesser on the high-yielding Mexican wheat varieties that had done well in field tests by young Pakistani scientists trained by Borlaug in Mexico. But the Mexican varieties needed heavy applications of fertilizer and modification of farmer's cultural practices. Pakistanis preferred white wheat, and Dr.

Borlaug and his colleagues at CIMMYT had developed a white-kernel variety related to the red-seeded Lerma Rojo 64. Norman told him about a meeting he had with Pakistani officials about Mexican wheat. Two Pakistani officials were trying to block the Mexican wheat program, arguing that "the Mexican wheats were the wrong color, taste bad, and they are too short-strawed; our cattle will starve because the wheat does not produce enough bousa (forage)." Norman argued that all the wheat in the Asian subcontinent used to be red, and in the previous two years, Pakistan had imported close to ten million tons of wheat from the United States—some from Canada and some from Australia. All the wheat from the United States and Canada were red, and Pakistanis ate it. Norman said, "It was an awful meeting. Everyone was mad." Then Leon Hesser learned that an enterprising Mexican farmer had obtained some seeds of the white-kernel wheat "and had proceeded surreptitiously to multiply it." West Pakistan's*[1] secretary of agriculture Amir Ahmed Khan asked if it might be possible to obtain some of that seed. Hesser wrote a justification for a $25,000 grant for fifty tons of the white seed from the Mexican farmer. The American ambassador approved it, and an American extension advisor, Staley Pitts, who was home on leave in Arizona, got the assignment to "get your ass down in Mexico," purchase fifty tons of the white wheat, and get it to West Pakistan in time to plant in fall. Staley flew to Mexico and purchased the white wheat from the farmer. The farmer agreed to deliver the wheat across the border into Arizona. Hesser wrote, "Staley knew better than to get tangled with Mexican officials in moving 'illicit' [my quotations] wheat across the border" (I guess we better not ask any questions about this). Staley called the wheat Mexipak, and the name stuck. Then Staley got two semitrailers to pick up the wheat at the border and hauled it to the port at Los Angeles. They arrived at the port during the weekend. An American cargo ship was departing from Los Angeles on Sunday evening with Karachi as one of its intended ports. But there were

---

1   Originally, there was West Pakistan and East Pakistan after Pakistan split from India in 1948. In 1972, after a war between India and West Pakistan, East Pakistan got its independence from West Pakistan and became Bangladesh.

no dock workers during the weekend. Staley called the president of the line and said, "We've got people starving in Pakistan, you must help us." And the wheat was loaded onto the ship before it departed Sunday evening. My hat's off to Staley Potts. I could never have accomplished such a feat!

When the wheat arrived at the port in Karashi, it was loaded onto army trucks and distributed to farmers across the Punjab with instructions on how to grow it. The seed multiplied manifold and was distributed widely.

Then the minister of agriculture of East Pakistan (now Bangladesh) travelled to Mexico to purchase a large amount of wheat. With Borlaug as interpreter, he announced that he would not purchase any Lerma Rojo 64 wheat until he had purchased 2,000 tons of the white wheat. The farmer who had "illicitly" obtained the white wheat offered only 500 tons. The minister refused. The other Mexican farmers were outraged that the farmer who had illicitly grown white wheat was holding up their business. After three hours of heated negotiations, the Minister agreed to purchase 1,700 tons of white wheat. He then purchased 40,000 tons of Lerma Rojo 64 wheat. It was the largest purchase of any grain by one country from another country in the history of agriculture.

In 1966, President Ayub Khan made the economic decision to commit his government to imports of fertilizer, to invest in a domestic fertilizer industry, and to provide credits to farmers for purchase of fertilizer and seed. He also assured farmers that they would receive a price for their wheat equivalent to the international market price.

With Dr. Ignacio (Nacho) Narvaez as Ford Foundation advisor on wheat production in Pakistan, extension advisors on the front lines, and a Ford Foundation economist—Norwegian Dr. Oddvack Aresvick—as consultant to the minister of agriculture, Khuda Bakhsh Bucha, Pakistan launched a national wheat production campaign in the fall of 1966. The 1967 harvest from fields planted to the Mexipak seed was excellent.

On March 8, 1968, William S. Gaud, administrator of the United States Agency for International Development, coined the phrase "the Green Revolution" in an address before an international group in Washington, DC. Pakistan achieved self-sufficiency in wheat production with the harvest of April 1968.

Borlaug's Mexican dwarf wheat and its Indian and Pakistani derivatives were the catalyst that launched the Green Revolution. By the spring of 1968, Dr. Borlaug was becoming known in Pakistan as the "father of the Green Revolution."

The Nobel Peace Prize

The 1970 Nobel Peace Prize was awarded to Dr. Norman Borlaug for his role in modernizing agriculture in the developing world—to provide bread for a hungry world. But when the award was announced on October 20, Borlaug was not at home; he had left early for the field. His wife, Margaret, got eight phone calls from Oslo, Norway, wanting to talk to Dr. Borlaug. When she asked if she could take a message, she was told "No, madam. I need to speak to him personally. It's an important matter, strictly private." Finally, on the sixth call, the caller identified himself as a reporter from an Oslo newspaper; he said the chairman of the Nobel Selection Committee was to announce that day that Dr. Norman Borlaug had been awarded the Nobel Peace Prize. She thought it may be a hoax, but after receiving two more calls, she was finally convinced that it must be true. She called the project office in Mexico City and arranged that a car and driver would pick her up and take her to the Toluca Agricultural Experiment Station. At the station, she was told that Norman was working at the far end of the station, and the station manager arranged for a driver to take her in a pickup truck. Norman was working with six young scientists, all in sweaty mud-stained clothes. They needed to select eight thousand wheat plants, thresh and pack the grain, and get to the Sonora experiment station by November 1 for planting in the winter nursery.

Norman was concerned when he saw Margaret. He thought something had happened to one of his elderly parents. She said, "Norman, you've been awarded the Nobel Peace Prize. I had a string of phone calls this morning from reporters of the Oslo newspaper *Aftenposten*." But Norman would not believe her. He said it had to be a hoax and wanted to go back to selecting wheat plants. While Margaret was trying to convince him that the news was true, another pickup truck arrived with six reporters with their cameras. The Mexico City press had gotten the news. Norman spent the rest of the day facing reporters and television cameras, giving interviews. His and Margaret's lives would never be the same. Norman was showered with telegrams and letters of congratulations from around the world—including Indian Prime Minister Indira Ghandi; President Ayub Khan of Pakistan; the president of the United States, Richard Nixon; Henry Ford; and the Rockefeller family.

CIMMYT

In 1963, Mexican president Adolfo Lopez Mateos made a trip to Southeast Asia. In the Philippines, he visited the new International Rice Research Institute (IRRI). Dr. Robert Chandler, the director general, informed him that IRRI was inspired by the Rockefeller Foundation program in Mexico.

Excited, Lopez Mateos, upon his return to Mexico, arranged a state dinner to thank Harrar, Wellhausen, Borlaug, and Niederhauser for their work. The next day, he met with George Harrar, who was then the president of the Rockefeller Foundation, and suggested that something similar to IRRI be established in Mexico, specializing in corn and wheat. Harrar discussed this idea with representatives of the Ford Foundation who agreed to join the Rockefeller Foundation to fund this international venture. The agreement was signed on October 25, 1963, with Mexico's minister of agriculture to establish the International Center for Maize and Wheat Improvement; in Spanish, it is El Centro Internacional de Mejoramiento de Maiz y Trigo (CIMMYT) with additional financial support from the US Agency for International Development (USAID), as well as the United Nations Development Program (UNDP), and the Inter-American Development Bank (IDB). Ed Wellhausen was appointed as the founding director of CIMMYT. The original board of trustees included such luminaries as George Harrar, president of the Rockefeller Foundation; Colombian Virgilio Barco, future ambassador to the United Nations and future president of Colombia; Galo Plaza, Ecuador's minister of agriculture, then president of Ecuador and later president of the Organization of American States (OAS); and Prince M. C. Chakabandhu, influential member of the royal family of Thailand who had advanced training in agriculture and other international luminaries.

CIMMYT was created as an autonomous international training institute with an international board of trustees and staff. Dr. Borlaug was made director of its International Wheat Improvement Program. There were three wheat research stations: one each at Chapingo and Toluca in the South and one in the Yaki Valley in the North. All data and materials would be made available worldwide to any country, free of charge. Within twenty years, the center had about 4,000 researchers from 120 countries. In 1983, Dr. Borlaug retired from the Rockefeller Foundation and CIMMYT at age sixty-five and was made a Lifetime Fellow by the Rockefeller Board of Trustees. He continued to consult for CIMMYT for nearly thirty years.

Africa

In the mid-1980s, when Dr. Bourlaug retired from the Rockefeller Foundation and was becoming a "senior statesman to the world's food community," Africa was identified as a great challenge. When colonialism ended in Africa in the 1960s, African farmers had ample food supplies. Some countries were exporting food. But during the 1970s, population growth started to outpace increases in food production. In the 1980s, some African countries started experiencing food shortages. Then the late Ryoichi Sasakawa, chairman of the Japan Shipbuilding Industry Foundation, called Norman Borlaug and asked him to start a Green Revolution in sub-Saharan Africa. At first, Norman said he had little knowledge of Africa, that he was semiretired and "too old to start learning now." Mr. Sasakawa told him "I'm thirteen years older than you are, Dr. Borlaug. We should have started sooner and didn't, so let's start tomorrow!" And Dr. Borlaug was recruited to fight hunger in Africa, which he did for the next twenty years. He organized a workshop in Geneva, Switzerland, to discuss the African problem. He invited fifty experts in agriculture, including many with experience in Africa. Former president Jimmy Carter was part of the team. The workshop identified the need to engage African farmers through agricultural extension education programs. A conclusion from the workshop was that the food crisis in Africa is the result of a longtime neglect of agriculture by political leaders. Most African governments gave agriculture a low priority. Norman identified the need for a network of roads as a high priority—roads so farmers could take their harvest to the markets. An improved basic transportation system would accelerate agricultural production, break down tribal animosities, and help establish rural schools and clinics in areas where teachers and health practitioners could not venture.

With Jimmy Carter's help, a partnership called Sasakawa Global 2000 was formed between the Sasakawa African Association and the Carter Center's Global 2000 program. In January 1986, Borlaug and Jimmy Carter visited several African countries, generating strong interest in action-oriented food crop projects. They started with development programs in Sudan and Ghana. Borlaug recruited a number of Mexican collaborators including Ignacio Narvaez and two African PhDs, Marcel Galiba of Senegal and Michael Foster of Ghana.

Dr. Borlaug's team went to work in early 1986 in Ghana and Sudan. Results of field plots of maize, sorghum, and wheat yields were two to three times higher than national averages. Farmers lined up to join the program. Projects were started eventually in fifteen African countries. During the last twenty years, as a result of Dr. Borlaug's efforts, yields of maize have at least doubled, often tripled, and sometimes quadrupled. His International Maize and Wheat Center produced genetically researched corn seeds that naturally tolerate the herbicide imazapyr. The corn seeds can be soaked in the herbicide, which kills the parasitic witchweed when it attempts to invade the roots of the corn plants.

On May 13, 2002, Norman Borlaug wrote in the *Wall Street Journal* an article about his efforts in Africa. He wrote, "low-yield farming is only sustainable for people with high death rates, and thanks to better medical care, more babies are surviving. . . . Africa desperately needs the simple, effective, high-yield farming systems that have made the First World's food supply safe and secure, and kept its wild species from extinction: chemical fertilizers, improved seeds bred for local conditions, and integrated pest management (with pesticides). Without the basics, Africa is likely to see tens of millions more undernourished children by 2020."

But something happened in Africa that hit an environmental manager like me deep in the heart. Environmental groups were successful, for a time, to block the use of chemical fertilizers in Borlaug's African projects. My environmental friends often focus fanatically on the word *chemical* and equate it with *toxic*. Let me clarify that the so-called chemical fertilizers consist of naturally occurring minerals, mixed in the right amounts to replenish the nutrients depleted from the soil. The most important element, nitrogen, is extracted from the air we breathe. Environmentalists insist that only organic (manure) fertilizers should be used. Borlaug correctly explained that we should use all available manure and other organic fertilizers. But it's not practical to depend on organic fertilizer for all the agricultural needs in Africa. There is not enough manure to supply fertilizer to all cultivated lands. It would require a larger number of cattle that would need a larger amount of land devoted to pastures instead of for planting food for people. The plants cannot differentiate between nitrogen and nutrients that came from organic or inorganic fertilizers. The nitrogen is absorbed in the same way from organic or inorganic sources. Borlaug also pointed out that by increasing the yield of existing farmland, his followers removed the necessity for destroying standing forests to clear additional farmland. A distinguished professor of the University of Manitoba, Vaclav Smil, said, "Without the 80 million tons of [nutrient] nitrogen consumed annually [from chemical fertilizers], the world could [feed] no more than four billion people, two billion fewer than inhabit the Earth today." Many of these environmentalists, said Borlaug, do their lobbying from comfortable offices in cities. They have never produced a ton of food. If they lived at least one month among the poor and starving peoples of the world, they would be screaming for chemical fertilizer, insecticides, and herbicides.

Genetic Engineering

To feed a growing world population, there are two options: The first is to cultivate more land, denying it to wild animal and plant species, including endangered species. The second is to produce more food from the land that is already being farmed. Genetic engineering involves gene-splicing to create new plants with highly specific characteristics. According to Borlaug, for ten thousand years, farmers have been genetically modifying the makeup of crops by selecting in wild populations of plants those of faster growth and better-tasting fruits. Most of our crops were generated from the cross-pollination done by Mother Nature. In the middle of the nineteenth century, Friar Gregor Mendel discovered the basic laws of inheritance. Then farmers and scientists began crossbreeding plant species to obtain plants that would resist illnesses and insects and produced better yields. Biotechnology had its origins in prehistoric times when microorganisms were used for fermentation. Brewing techniques for beer were referred to as zymotechnology. The production of penicillin from cultures of the fungus *Pencillium notatum* during World War II is another example of biotechnology.

Genetic engineering originated with the discovery of the recombinant DNA technique by Cohen and Boyer in 1973 by which a section of DNA was cut from the plasmid of an *E. coli* bacterium and transferred into the DNA of another. In principle, this enabled bacteria to adopt the genes and produce proteins of other organisms, including humans. This is referred to as the new biotechnology.

Biotechnology, or transgenic research, has resulted in improvements of maize and cotton to control insect pests without the use of chemical insecticides. Genes have been incorporated into soybean varieties to facilitate weed control. Borlaug dreamed of using transgenic research to transfer to wheat the resistance of rice to all types of rust: stem, stripe, and leaf. According to Borlaug, genetic modification can speed up the process to provide food for the world's rapidly expanding population.

Critics are concerned that the environmental and health effects of genetically modified crops could have adverse effects. But examples of the beneficial effects of genetically engineered food abound. A genetically engineered variety of rice called "golden rice" has a higher level of vitamin A, which reduces blindness and would boost the health of poor people in developing countries. It would boost the productivity of unskilled workers in Asia.

But environmental groups, including Greenpeace, claim that biotech crops would poison people, create new food allergies, and unleash "superweeds" that can overwhelm the environment. The European Union officially blocked imports of biotech commodities for several years. Fear is a primary weapon of the antibiotech activists. European activists told African governments that American corn containing the Bt gene was poisonous. This is the same corn extensively consumed in the United States. The president of Zambia ordered thousands of tons of American corn banned from his country despite a food crisis. Yet agricultural biotechnology has received greater scientific scrutiny than any other farming technology. According to the National Academy of Sciences in 2004, "to date, no adverse health effect attributed to genetic engineering has been documented in the human population." The most prestigious national academies of science in North America and Europe support genetic engineering to improve quantity, quality, and availability of food supplies. As of December 2004, Europe, where resistance to biotechnology has been stiffest, was gradually accepting bioengineered foods. The European Union ended a six-year moratorium by approving imports of two bioengineered varieties of corn.

At Nairobi, Kenya, in 2000, Norman Borlaug defended the utilization of genetically modified organisms (GMO) to boost production in the world. He told a forum of researchers and food scientists at the Nairobi International Center for Research in Agriculture and Forestry that such organisms could play a key role in bringing about food security. "There is no evidence to indicate that biotechnology is dangerous. After all, mother nature has been doing this kind of thing for God knows how long," he said. "We need sophisticated scientific technology to boost our production." He said zero risk is a nonissue where only plant genes are concerned and not chemicals. "Zero risk is something that does not exist and not tenable in a biological world where things keep on changing." He said Africa is undergoing instability because there is not enough food to feed the people. "We need more investments in agriculture and we must stop looking at agriculture as a donkey's profession." Borlaug challenged African leaders to embark on productive technology that would ensure predictable food supply to their masses.

The Distinguished College Professor

When Norman Borlaug retired from CIMMYT's international wheat program in 1979 at the age of sixty-five, several universities tried to recruit him as a distinguished professor. CIMMYT also wanted him to serve as their consultant. He gave lectures and seminars at the University of Minnesota (his alma mater), Cornell University, the University of Florida, Auburn University, and finally, Texas A&M as distinguished professor of international agriculture. For the next twenty years, Professor Borlaug taught in the fall semester at Texas A&M, teaching courses on food, population, the environment, forestry, and wildlife. In 1999, Texas A&M dedicated a new science building: Norman E. Borlaug Center for Southern Crop Improvement, a well-equipped plant biotechnology research center.

The End of a Great Life

Norman's wife, Margaret, died in 2006 after complications from a fall. Norman died on September 12, 2009, of cancer.

On September 7, 2010, an article in the public health blog *The Pump Handle*, entitled "Are More Food Crises on the Way?" by Liz Borowski, mentions the global food crisis of 2008 caused by poor wheat harvests in Europe, the United States, and Australia that led to a shortfall in global supplies. Grain became more expensive, so poorer countries could not afford it. Russia, as a result of a drought in the summer of 2010, has banned exports of its wheat. The International Water Management Institute released a report about millions of farmers' vulnerability to erratic rainfall, something that can worsen as climate disruption continues. Water harvesting is one of the options being tested with mixed results in several developing countries. In conclusion, there are still many challenges for hunger fighters worldwide in years to come. We will miss Norman Borlaug, but hopefully, other scientists will rise to the challenge, inspired by Norman's life, and continue his fight.

Richard Feynman
Physicist, Genius, and a Very Funny Curious Character

If your idea of a genius scientist or theoretical physicist who helped develop the atomic bomb and later won the Nobel Prize for Physics is a very dull, nerdish person, then you'll be happy to learn that Richard Feynman does not fit that mold. Eccentric, yes—he wrote an autobiographical book entitled *"Surely You're Joking, Mr. Feynman!": Adventures of a Curious Character.* The origin of the title was his first day at Princeton University where he was invited to a tea hosted by the dean of the graduate college. Feynman admitted in his book that he did not even know what a tea was; he had no social abilities whatsoever. When the wife of the dean asked, "Would you like cream or lemon in your tea, Mr. Feynman?" he replied, "I'll have both, thank you." Suddenly, he heard "Heh-heh-heh-heh-heh. Surely you're joking, Mr. Feynman?" And that was his first experience with "this tea business."

But let's go back a few years. Richard Feynman was born in 1918 in a small town called Far Rockaway in New York. As a child, he liked to tinker with electrical gadgets. Once, he invented a burglar alarm that scared the daylights out of his parents when they came home late at night, and the thing went *bong, bong, bong!*

He did his undergraduate degree at the Massachusetts Institute of Technology (MIT), the school for brilliant minds. He admitted in his autobiography that at MIT, he was interested only in science; he was good at nothing else. But he was required to take courses in English and two electives in humanities. He was able to take a course of astronomy that, incredibly, was listed as a humanities course. But in English and in a philosophy elective, he had to fake and write some crazy things in his term papers that miraculously got him passing grades. For his term paper in the philosophy class, he had to answer the question "How does the stream of consciousness end when you go to sleep?" The idea for this came when he remembered a problem that his father had given him: Supposing Martians came to Earth and they did not have to sleep—what if a Martian asked him, "How does it feel to go to sleep?" For four weeks, as he went to sleep, he wrote "observations" of what happened as he fell asleep. Then he wrote a paper explaining the observations he made and explained that all observations were made while he was watching himself fall asleep but did not know what it was like to fall asleep while he was not watching himself. He described his philosophy professor reading his paper sounding like:

> Uh wugga wuh. Uh wugga whu
> Uh wugga wugga wugga

In other words, he had no clue what the professor was saying. But I guess he passed the course.

For his senior thesis at MIT, Feynman was given a problem: why does quartz expand so little when heated? Metals have a "coefficient of expansion"—that is, when heated (energy added), their molecules are agitated and the substance expands. But quartz expanded very little compared to other substances. Feynman used quantum mechanics to explain the phenomenon. His thesis evolved beyond the problem that his thesis advisor had assigned him. He titled his thesis "Forces and Stresses in Molecules." Quantum mechanics explain the behavior of matter and its interactions with energy at the level of atoms and subatomic particles. Quantum mechanics can explain phenomena in materials science. Classic mechanics could not explain how electrons could arrange themselves in an atom; the negatively charged electrons must seek a state of lowest energy. Under classical mechanics, the electrons would spiral toward the positively charged nuclei, and substance itself would vanish. Quantum mechanics would give the electron "a definite point like position." But the calculations to determine the forces working on a nucleus were very laborious and time-consuming. Feynman found a better method to calculate the force for a given configuration. His method caused sensation among the MIT physics faculty. Feynman's method "permitted considerable saving of labor of calculations" as Feynman remarked. Professor John C. Slater, Feynman's thesis advisor and a leading physicist, had Feynman write a shortened version that was published in *Physical Review* with the also-shortened title of "Forces in Molecules."

When he finished his bachelor of science at MIT in 1939, he loved the place so much that he wanted to go to graduate school there. But when he told Professor Slater of his desire to stay at MIT, Professor Slater told him "We won't let you in here." When Feynman told Professor Slater that he thought MIT was the best school for science in the country, the professor told him "That's why you should go to some other school. You should find out how the rest of the world is."

And so Feynman went to Princeton. His classmates at MIT—upon hearing of his plans since Princeton is an elegant university, an imitation of an English school, and Feynman being so rough around the edges—made jokes such as "Wait till they see the mistake they made." So Feynman decided to try to be nice when he got to Princeton. And I already told you how he made the wife of the dean of the graduate college at Princeton, Mrs. Eisenhart, laugh on his first day there when she asked him if he wanted lemon or cream in his tea. Soon, Feynman learned that when he heard Mrs. Eisenhart go "Heh-heh-heh-heh-heh," it meant "error," and he'd better get it straightened out.

Feynman wrote that at Princeton they wore academic gowns to dinner. This scared the life out of him the first night because he hated formality. But then he learned that it was convenient because students, after playing tennis, could put the gown over the sweaty tennis clothes and go to dinner without having to change or shower (I'm glad I never had to sit next to one of those guys at dinner!). And there was a rule that you never cleaned the gown. So the first-year students had nice gowns, but by the time they were about to finish their PhDs after the third year, the gowns were literally rags hanging from their shoulders (you know, somehow I find this story a bit difficult to believe).

The first thing Feynman wanted to see at Princeton was the cyclotron. A cyclotron is a circular particle accelerator where charged particles accelerate outward from the center along a spiral path; it has applications in particle physics research and nuclear medicine. There were a lot of scientific papers published about research done with the Princeton cyclotron. He was amazed when he was told that the cyclotron was in the basement of the physics building. When he saw it, he realized why Princeton was the perfect place for him. There were wires strung all over the place, switches hanging from the wires, cooling water dripping from the valves—"it was the most god awful mess you ever saw." It was complete, absolute chaos (I would have hated it). It reminded him of his lab at home. Feynman wrote that there was a fire in the room because of all the wires, and it destroyed the cyclotron. Oh well, this was decades before the Occupational Safety and Health Administration was created and safety became law.

While a graduate student at Princeton, Feynman was a research assistant to Professor John Wheeler. Feynman worked on a problem that electrons don't act on themselves; they only act on other electrons. Feynman explained the problems in his own words:

> When you shake an electron, it irradiates energy and so there's a loss. That means there must be a force on it. And there must be a different force when it's charged than when it's not charged. (If the force were exactly the same when it was charged and not charged, in one case it would lose energy, and in the other it wouldn't. You can't have two different answers to the same problem).

I hope that you understood all that.

Professor Wheeler liked the concept, and he and Feynman immersed themselves in analysis using the quantum theory of electrodynamics. Then Wheeler told Feynman that he should give a seminar on this problem in order for Feynman to gain experience giving talks. Wheeler would work out the quantum theory part and give a seminar on that later. This would be Feynman's first technical talk. Wheeler arranged for physicist Eugene Wigner to put it on the regular seminar schedule.

A couple of days later, Wigner told Feynman that because the subject of the seminar was so interesting, he had invited the famous astronomer Norris Russell. Also, the famous mathematician John von Neumann would be attending. Also, the famous physicist Wolfgang Pauli, who was visiting from Switzerland, would be attending. By this time, Feynman was turning yellow. Then Wigner said, "Professor Einstein only rarely comes to our weekly seminars, but your work is so interesting that I've invited him specially, so he's coming too." Feynman turned green. Wigner tried to calm him by explaining that if Professor Russell falls asleep—and he probably would—it did not mean that the seminar is bad; he fell asleep in all seminars. If Professor Pauli was nodding all the time it did not mean that he was in agreement; he nodded because he had palsy.

Feynman told Wheeler of all the famous scientists that would be attending the seminar and how uneasy he felt. Wheeler told him not to worry; he would answer all the questions.

The day of the seminar, Feynman was the first in the room, writing equations on the board, when Einstein came in and said pleasantly, "Hello, I'm coming to your seminar. But first, where is the tea?" Feynman directed him to the tea and continued writing equations.

When Feynman started his talk, his hands were shaking. But then he calmed down and focused on his physics topic. At the end of the talk, Professor Pauli stood up and said, "I do not think that this theory can be right" because of this and this and this. Then he turned to Einstein and said, "Don't you agree, Professor Einstein?" But Einstein, in his pleasant German voice, said "Nooooo" in a very polite voice. He said the theory was possible even if it conflicted with the theory of gravitational interaction, which was not so well established. Einstein was very open-minded with new theories and very patient with young scientists. But neither Wheeler nor Feynman was able to solve a quantum theory of half-advanced, half-retarded potentials, whatever that means.

World War II Patriotic Work

In the summer of 1941, before America's entry into World War II, the federal government started hiring physicists for war-related work. The government created the Office of Scientific Research and Development. Feynman had been offered a summer job at Bell Labs, but when an army general came looking for two physicists for work at Frankford Arsenal near Philadelphia, Feynman—full of patriotism—turned down Bell Labs and went to work at Frankford. Regretfully, he was assigned to work on a primitive analog computer to aim artillery pieces. He regretted turning down Bell Labs.

After his summer job at Frankford, Feynman returned to Princeton to write his doctoral thesis. Then professor Robert Wilson visited him one day and, confidentially, told him a secret. The British were working on a separation of uranium-235 (fissionable) from uranium-238 (nonfissionable). The codename was *tubealloy*. The Americans were building a nuclear reactor. Wilson was assembling a team of instructors, graduate students, and engineers to work on the uranium separation project. He wanted Feynman in his team. He invited Feynman to attend a meeting where he would present the project to the other instructors and students. But Feynman turned him down. He was busy with his thesis and was disillusioned with his job at the Franklin Arsenal. Wilson asked him to at least attend the meeting. Feynman attended and was unable to go back to his thesis.

So Feynman was eventually recruited to work at the Manhattan Project. He started at Princeton, working as one of two theoreticians—himself and a graduate student of mathematics, Paul Olum—in Professor Wilson's project. This project was supposed to develop a "blast gauge for measuring explosive pressure" and a dull-sounding investigation of the thermal properties of graphite (later, Feynman found out that this involved the thermal-neutron properties of a material destined for nuclear reactors). The apparatus they were developing was "one ungainly tube the length of an automobile, spouting smaller tubes and electrical wiring." Wilson called his apparatus an *isotron* (his competitor, Ernest Lawrence, called his a *calutron [California University + tron]*). It was supposed to work like this according to James Gleick's book:

The isotron first vaporized and ionized chunks of uranium—heated them until they gave up an electron and thus became electrically charged. Then a magnetic field set them in motion. The stream of atoms passed through a hole that organized it into a tight beam.

The idea was to put oscillations in the magnetic field that would make the atoms of U-235 and U-238 separate in different directions and into separate containers. Sounds simple . . . but it was not! Feynman and Olum thought that Wilson's idea was somewhere between possible and hopeless. In their calculations, they had to resort to guesswork and approximation. There were complications. Lawrence, at Berkeley, was their project's worst enemy. He wanted to absorb the isotron into his project, shut down the Princeton group, and take its staff and equipment for his *calutron*. He eventually succeeded, and the Princeton group was shut down.

In the spring of 1942, Professor Wheeler advised Feynman to finish his doctoral thesis no matter how many questions remained open. Feynman's thesis created a new quantum electrodynamics. Feynman wrote a conclusion with a list of the flaws in his thesis. He was not satisfied with the physical meaning of his equations; he felt they lacked clear interpretation. But his official thesis readers, Wheeler and Wigner, were not concerned by that. In June, Princeton awarded Feynman his doctoral degree.

Now he was ready to get married. But his fiancée, Arline, had tuberculosis. His parents were concerned for his health and opposed the marriage. So Feynman and Arline crossed New York Harbor on the Staten Island Ferry and married in a city office on Staten Island with no family or friends present, only two strangers as witnesses. Then Feynman drove Arline to her new home, a charity hospital in Brown Mills, New Jersey. Then in the winter of 1943, physicist Robert Oppenheimer (who would be known after the war as the father of the atomic bomb), the director of Los Alamos Laboratory, called Feynman long-distance from Chicago to inform him that he had found a sanatorium for Arline in Albuquerque. And by doing so, Oppenheimer bound Feynman to him.

On December 2, 1942, at a squash court at the University of Chicago, Enrico Fermi and his team conducted the first critical nuclear chain reaction in his pile of graphite blocks, cylinders of uranium, a cadmium rod, a safety rod called ZIP, boron trifluoride counters to measure neutron intensities, and ionization chambers for higher neutron intensities. When Fermi announced "The pile has gone critical" if left uncontrolled for an hour and a half, the release of energy would have been a million kilowatts. It would have killed everyone in the room and melted down. It would have been like a Chernobyl accident in the middle of Chicago. But Fermi ordered ZIP in and shut down the reaction. "Men had controlled the release of energy from the atomic nucleus."

At Los Alamos, Oppenheimer had put Hans Bethe, the famous nuclear physicist, in charge of the Theoretical Division. And there, Bethe met Feynman. When other physicists heard Bethe's booming laughter, they knew that Feynman was nearby. Bethe and Feynman, a strange pair, were nicknamed "Battleship" and "Mosquito Boat." Bethe would plow slowly forward while Feynman would buzz back and forth, across his bow, yelling "You're crazy" or "That's nuts." He patiently explained his idea again and would say, "No, you're wrong." Bethe appreciated Feynman's criticism because he would find flaws before the idea went too far. So Bethe made Feynman, then twenty-five, a team leader. This was a job normally reserved for prominent physicists.

Trouble with the Censors

Now, because of the highly classified work being done at Los Alamos, the army did not want people, especially those crazy scientists, to write to friends and family telling them all they were doing. So they censored the mail. Feynman thought that it was "utterly illegal" to censor the mail of people inside the United States. It was set up as "voluntary" where the employees would agree not to seal the envelopes of their letters and agree for censors to read their letters. Also, they would agree to let censors read letters that were sent to them. If there was something in the letters that the censors did not like, the censor would send the letter back to the sender with a note that something violated a paragraph in their security agreement. So Feynman, with his father and his wife, started a game to drive the censors crazy. His father and wife would send him letters with codes. When the censors asked what they meant, Feynman told them he did not have the key for the codes because the idea was for him to decipher the codes. So the censors demanded that his father and wife include the key for the codes for the censors to keep and be able to read the codes. One day, his wife sent a letter with a list that said, "litharge, glycerin, etc." The censors removed the list, claiming it was a code without the key. But his wife explained it was a list of ingredients she needed to make a cement to fix an onyx box.

On an occasion, Feynman got a letter from his wife saying that she did not feel comfortable writing because the "_____" was looking over her shoulder. There was a space (_____) where ink eradicator was used. Feynman complained to the censors that nothing was supposed to be removed from the letters according to the agreement. The censors explained that there was supposed to be no reference to censorship in the letters. Also, they denied that they used ink eradicator; they were supposed to cut the word out with scissors. Feynman was told to tell his wife not to use the word *censor* in her letters. But when Feynman wrote to his wife to tell her this, the word *censor* was cut off from his letter. So he had to visit his wife in person to tell her this.

On another occasion, his wife found an ad in a magazine about writing a letter to a boyfriend in a jigsaw puzzle—so she did. But the censors sent a note to Feynman that said "We do not have time to play games. Please instruct your wife to confine herself to ordinary letters." I would have been a bit aggravated myself.

Keeping the Oak Ridge Plant from Exploding

There were two important industrial facilities involved in the making of the atomic bomb: Los Alamos would make the bomb, but the plant at Oak Ridge, Tennessee, was to separate the isotopes of uranium-235 (the explosive one) from uranium-238 (this was most of the uranium that was not fissionable, so it could not be used in the bomb). The physicists at Los Alamos kept sending instructions to Oak Ridge on how to "assay" the uranium—that is, to determine how much U-235 was in it—but they never got it right. One of the physicists that worked on fission with Enrico

Fermi, Emilio Segre, decided he needed to go to Oak Ridge to see what they were doing. But the army would not let him go, arguing that they wanted to keep information on how to make the bomb at Los Alamos and out of Oak Ridge. The Oak Ridge scientists and engineers only knew they were separating U-235 from U-238 but did not know what for. Finally, Segre was able to convince the army that if Oak Ridge could not separate the U-235 correctly, there would be no bomb. When he got to Oak Ridge, he found that they were wheeling a carboy of "green water" (uranium nitrate solution). When he asked them if they were planning to handle it like that when it was purified, they said, "Sure, why not?" Segre asked, "Won't it explode?" The Oak Ridge guys said, "Huh! *Explode?*" The army said, "You see! We shouldn't have let any information get to them, now they are all upset!" (Does that make sense to you?) It happened that the army had figured out how many kilograms of U-235 were needed to make a bomb (sounds like they were spying on Los Alamos) and determined that there would never be that much at Oak Ridge, so no danger. The problem was that neutrons were enormously more effective when slowed down in water; it would take a hundredth as much material to make a reaction that would produce radioactivity that would kill people around. It was *very* dangerous.

So Oppenheimer directed Segre to go through the entire plant and find where all the concentrations were. Los Alamos would calculate "how much material can come together before there's an explosion." So a scientist called Robert Christy and his group did calculations for water solutions and Feynman's group did calculations for dry powder in boxes, and they calculated how much material they could calculate safely. Christy was going to visit Oak Ridge and explain the situation to them. Feynman gave Christy his calculations. But Christy got pneumonia, so Feynman had to go to Oak Ridge. Before he went, Oppenheimer told him to make sure certain technically able people would attend his meeting, and he gave him a list of names. Feynman asked, "What if they're not in the meeting? What am I supposed to do?" Oppenheimer said, "Then you should say, 'Los Alamos cannot accept the responsibility for the safety of the Oak Ridge plant unless ——'" Feynman said "You mean me, little Richard, is going to go in there and say ——?" Oppenheimer said, "Yes, little Richard, you go and do that." Feynman had to grow up really fast.

But when he got to the plant, all the big shots and the technical people were there. A lieutenant, Zumwalt, escorted him everywhere he went. The lieutenant told Feynman that he should not explain to the Oak Ridge people how the neutrons worked for security reasons. Feynman argued that the Oak Ridge people would not be able to understand all the rules about not accumulating material if they did not understand the scientific reasons. Then Feynman repeated Oppenheimer's words: "Los Alamos cannot accept responsibility for the safety of the Oak Ridge plant unless they are fully informed as to how it works!" So Lieutenant Zumwalt took Feynman to his colonel who said "Just five minutes" and went to the window to think. Feynman wrote, "I have a great deal of respect for these military guys, because I never can decide anything very important in any length of time at all." After five minutes, the colonel said, "All right Mr. Feynman, go ahead."

So Feynman explained to the Oak Ridge people how neutrons worked and how, if there were too many neutrons together, there can be trouble, so you have to keep material apart, etc. All this was elemental at Los Alamos, but at Oak Ridge, they had never heard about it. So they thought Feynman was a genius.

The Oak Ridge engineers decided to form groups to learn doing their own calculations and to properly design a safe plant to handle the separated material. They told Feynman to return in a few months to review the plans for the new plant. When the engineers started to explain what all these engineering drawings were and how the processes worked, Feynman was worried that he could not understand the symbols. There was one symbol—a square with a little cross in the middle—that was all over the drawings. Feynman was not sure if it was a valve or a window. So he pointed to one of those and asked, "What if this valve gets stuck?" He expected the engineers to say "It's not a valve but a window." But the engineers started to explain what would happen if the valve (it was a valve, after all) got stuck, something we now call process hazard analysis (PHA). Suddenly, the two engineers looked at each other and told Feynman "You are absolutely right, sir!" They had found a flaw in the design. Lieutenant Zumwalt said, "You're a genius. I got the idea you were a genius when you went through the plant once and could tell them about evaporator C-21 in building 90-207 the next morning. But what you have just done is so fantastic. I want to know how do you do that?" Feynman confessed he just wanted to know if the graphic was a valve or a window.

Arline's Death

Toward the end of the war, Arline, his wife, sick with tuberculosis, deteriorated badly. Feynman borrowed a car from his friend Klaus Fuchs (he was a Soviet spy, but nobody knew that) to visit his wife at the sanatorium at Albuquerque. Feynman picked up two hitchhikers, suspecting that he would need their help if he had car trouble. Sure enough, they had flat tires. The hitchhikers helped him fix the first flat tire. When the second tire went flat, they helped him push the car to a service station and helped him get a new tire. When they got the third flat tire, thirty miles away from Albuquerque, having no spare (tires were difficult to get during the war), they had to leave the car by the side of the road and hitchhike to Albuquerque. Arline died a few hours after he got to the hospital. The clock by her bedside (that he had given to her seven years earlier) had stopped at 9:22, the time on her death certificate! Feynman did something to himself psychologically; he put on a brave face and immersed himself in his work. He did not cry until several months later when he was walking by a department-store window with dresses and he thought that Arline would like one of them.

Advising Niels Bohr

The famous Danish physicists Niels Bohr and his son, Aage, would come to Los Alamos periodically to talk with the scientists. The Bohrs were so famous that scientists treated them as gods. The first time Feynman attended one of his meetings, he could barely see Niels Bohr's head as he walked among other scientists. For security reasons, Niels went by Nicholas Baker and Aage by

Jake Baker. The next time the Bohrs were scheduled to visit Los Alamos, Feynman got a phone call that went like this:

"Hello, Feynman?"
"Yes."
"This is Jake Baker." It was the son. "My father and I would like to speak to you."
"Me? I'm Feynman, I'm just a . . ." (I guess he was going to say he was Mr. Nobody or something like that).
"That's right. Is eight o'clock OK?"

So at eight o'clock, little Mr. "Nobody" Feynman got to visit with the world famous Niels and Aage Bohr. Aage said they had been thinking of how to make the bomb more efficient, and they explained their idea. Feynman said "No, it's not going to work. It's not efficient" and explained why not. Then Aage asked, how about so and so? Feynman said, "That sounds a little better, but it's got this damn fool idea in it." And so they went for about two hours discussing lots of ideas. Niels kept lighting his pipe that kept going off. When he talked, he mumbled, so Feynman had trouble understanding him. He could understand the son better. Finally, Niels said, "I guess we can call in the big shots now." So the great Los Alamos scientists were allowed to come in, and they discussed the ideas. Aage explained to Feynman that Niels told his son "Remember the name of the little fellow in the back over there? He's the only one that's not afraid of me and will say when I got a crazy idea." Niels knew that the other scientists would agree with anything he said even if it was not a good idea. So he wanted to talk to Feynman first (I bet you it was Hans Bethe who recommended Feynman to Dr. Bohr). Sometimes, it pays not to be a yes-man . . . but it's better to be more tactful than Feynman.

The Test of the Atomic Bomb

So in 1945 while Feynman was on vacation, visiting his parents, he got a message that said "The baby is expected on such and such a day." That was code meaning the date scheduled to test the atomic bomb. Robert Oppenheimer called the test Trinity (afterward, he could not remember why he called it that). Feynman returned to Los Alamos as the buses were leaving for the Trinity site. He and the others were twenty miles away from where the bomb would explode. They were issued dark glasses. Feynman thought that he would not be able to see anything with the dark glasses. He figured that the only thing that could hurt the eyes was ultraviolet radiation (bright light cannot do permanent damage to your eyes). He decided that instead of wearing the dark glasses, he would get behind the windshield of a truck (UV cannot penetrate glass).

Then there was this tremendous flash—so bright that he ducked. When he looked up, he saw the white light turning into yellow and then into orange. He wrote, "Finally a big ball of orange, the center of that was so bright, becomes a ball of orange that starts to rise and billow—a little bit and get a little black around the edges and then you see it's a big ball of smoke with flashes on the inside of the fire going out the heat." He claimed that he was "about the only guy who actually looked at the damn thing." He thought that since that other people had dark glasses, they probably saw very little. Also, they were told to lie on the floor. After about a minute and a half, there was a tremendous *bang* then rumble. Then they all knew that the bomb had worked. A man next to Feynman asked, "What was that?" Feynman replied, "That was the bomb."

At Los Alamos, Feynman had the job of taking a correspondent around Los Alamos to write an article. There was a room where there was a small silver-plated ball on a pedestal. It was plutonium, a new element that was made by man. The Nagasaki bomb was a plutonium bomb (the Hiroshima bomb was a uranium bomb, but it was difficult to separate the fissionable U-235 from the nonfissionable U-238). Plutonium is made by bombarding U-238 with neutrons; when an atom of U-238 captures a neutron, its atomic weight increases to 239, becoming plutonium (it's a little more complicated than that, but this is a simple explanation). But the funny thing was that the doorstop of the room where the plutonium was kept was made of gold. The scientists had done an experiment to see how many neutrons were reflected by different materials. They tested platinum, zinc, brass, and gold.

They had several pieces of gold, and somebody had the clever idea to make a doorstop made of gold. I wonder if it is still in Los Alamos.

After the war, Feynman went to Cornell University to teach. He poured his energy into a course of mathematical physics. He redesigned the course from the bottom up. In a radio show, he correctly told the audience that nuclear-powered cars would not be feasible because the gamma radiation emitted by the fission of uranium would kill the driver. The US Air Force, years later, would come to the same conclusion about nuclear-powered aircraft.

He had a hard time being a twenty-seven-year-old professor at Cornell. Most students thought that he was a freshman. Once, at a dance, he noticed that young women would dance with him, but when he asked them to dance again, they gave him excuses. Then one young lady, while dancing with him, asked him the same questions that the others had asked, "What are you?" "I'm a professor." "Professor of what?" "Theoretical physics." "Did you work on the atomic bomb?" "Yes, I was at Los Alamos during the war." "You're a damn liar," she said and walked off. Then he understood that he looked too young to be a professor who had worked on the atomic bomb during the war.

But after Los Alamos, the new professor of physics at Cornell was trying to find an area of physics where he could make a contribution to peacetime physics. He had a problem doing research at Cornell. He was not interested; he could not do research! He felt that he had burned himself out during the war. He was getting great job offers from other universities and from industry. There was a great offer from the Institute of Advanced Studies at Princeton. He turned them all down. He felt that he could not deliver what was expected of him. Professor Robert Wilson called him to his office and told him "Feynman, you are teaching your classes well; you're doing a good job, and we're very satisfied . . . But you shouldn't worry about what you are doing or not doing." That released him from feeling guilt.

A few days later, he saw in the cafeteria a guy fooling around, throwing a plate in the air. The plate wobbled as it went up in the air. Feynman noticed that the Cornell medallion on the plate went around faster than the wobbling. He analyzed the motion of the rotating plate; when the angle was very light, the medallion rotated twice as fast as the wobbling rate. He worked the calculations, and it came out as a complicated equation. He showed the calculations to Hans Bethe who asked him, "But what's the importance of it? Why are you doing it?" Feynman replied, "Hah! There's no importance whatsoever. I'm just doing it for the fun of it." He decided to enjoy physics and do whatever he liked. Through the years, he worked on many problems for fun from wobbles to electron orbits in relativity, the Dirac equation, and quantum electrodynamics. And ultimately, he was awarded a Nobel Prize that came from piddling around with the wobbling plate.

James Gleick wrote in the section "Alas, the Love of Women!":

> Since Arline's death he had pursued women with a single-mindedness that violated most of the public, if not the private, scruples associated with sexual ballet. He dated undergraduates, paid prostitutes in whorehouses, taught himself (as he saw it) how to beat bar girls at their own game, and slept with the young wives of several of his friends among the physics graduate students. . . . Love seemed almost a myth . . . What he had felt for Arlene he seemed to have placed on a shelf out of the way. . . . On professional trips overseas he seduced women so regularly that his hosts knew he expected them to make introductions.

He surprised his friends when he married Mary Louise Bell of Neodesha, Kansas, whom he met at a Cornell cafeteria. His friends considered her a platinum blonde ("the girl with the cellophane hair"). She wanted him to dress better. She told him that she did not usually think that scientists were much fun. She studied the history of Mexican art and textiles. While Feynman was teaching at a university in Brazil, she taught courses at Michigan State University in the History of Furniture and Institutional Interiors to men pursuing careers in hotel and restaurant management. Sometimes, she thought that she was married to an uneducated man with a PhD. They divorced nearly four years later.

The Woman in the Blue Bikini

In 1958, before bikini swimsuits became popular in the United States, Feynman noticed a beautiful young British woman in a blue bikini on the beach at Lake Genoa. He sat next to her and started a conversation. Feynman was in Geneva for a United Nations conference on the peaceful uses of atomic energy. Her name was Gweneth Howard, an Englishwoman who was seeing Europe by working as an au pair (household). He took her to a night club that night. He had been having a "sporadic and tempestuous" love affair with the wife of a research fellow. But the affair was coming to an end. Gweneth was twenty-four, and Feynman was forty. He invited her to come to California to be his maid for a salary of twenty dollars a week. At first, she refused; she was engaged to marry another man, but when that fell through, Gweneth agreed to immigrate to California with Feynman. He consulted a lawyer who advised him that "there were dangers in transporting women for immoral purposes." Feynman had a friend sign their papers as a third-party employer. Finally, in 1959, her visa came through, and Gweneth joined Feynman. Although they tried to keep the image that theirs was an employer-employee relationship, it became obvious to his friends that the relationship had turned romantic. They married on September 24, 1960. In 1962, their son, Carl, was born. Six years later, they adopted a daughter, Michelle.

The Nobel Prize

&&At 4:00 a.m. on November 21, 1965, a correspondent of the American Broadcasting Corporation was the first to call Feynman to inform him that he had won the Nobel Prize for Physics. He told Gweneth, but she thought he was joking. The phone kept ringing until they left it off the hook. Then at 9:00 a.m., a Western Union Telefax arrived naming Feynman, Schwinger, and Tomonaga the winners for their "fundamental work in quantum electrodynamics with deep-ploughing consequences for the physics of elementary particles." Several correspondents from various publications came to his home to interview him. They kept asking what he did to win the prize. The problem was that quantum electrodynamics is so complex that it was impossible to explain it in terms they could understand. Feynman replied, "Listen, buddy, if I could tell you in a minute what I did, it wouldn't be worth the Nobel Prize." For weeks, he worried about a rumor that after he accepted the prize from the king of Sweden, he could not turn his back on the king and would have to walk backward up a flight of stairs. A friend sent him an automobile rearview mirror as a joke. When the Swedish ambassador paid him a courtesy visit and Feynman confessed his worry, the ambassador assured him that he could face any direction—"No one climbed stairs backwards."

The 1965 Nobel Prize in Physics was shared by Sin-Itiro Tomonaga of Tokyo University of Education, Julian Schwinger of Harvard University, and Richard Feynman of the California Institute of Technology for advancing the theory quantum electrodynamics. An article in the Internet entitled "Introduction to quantum mechanics" defines quantum mechanics as "the body of scientific principles that explains the behavior of matter and its interaction on the scale of atoms and subatomic particles and how these phenomena could be related to everyday life." It states that "towards the end of the 19th century, scientists discovered phenomena . . . that classical physics could not explain." Quantum mechanics explained this phenomenon. It quotes Richard Feynman as saying quantum mechanics deals with "nature as she is absurd." Tomonaga and Schwinger solved discrepancies in the first relative theory in 1948 "by so called renormalization and consequently contributed to a new quantum electrodynamics." Feynman, also in 1948, "introduced so called Feynman diagrams, a graphical representation of interactions between different particles. These diagrams facilitate calculations of interaction probabilities."

At Sweden, during the king's dinner, Feynman got in trouble with a Swedish princess. She asked what his specialty was, and when he said "Physics," she said, "Oh well, nobody knows anything about that, so I guess we can't talk about it." Feynman replied, "On the contrary, it's because somebody knows something about it that we can't talk about physics. It's the things that nobody knows anything about that we can discuss." Then he went on to mention things such as weather, psychology, even international finance that people should not discuss because everyone knew all about it. Well, the princess obviously did not find it funny because her face froze, and she turned to talk to someone else and ignored him. Luckily for the United States, Feynman never became an ambassador.

The Space Shuttle Challenger Disaster

On January 28, 1986, the Space Shuttle Challenger exploded over the Atlantic seventy-three seconds after liftoff, killing the crew of seven astronauts—including Christa McAuliff, the "Teacher in Space." President Ronald Reagan appointed an independent commission to investigate the accident, which included a Nobel Prize winner scientist: Richard Feynman. He was included in the list of suggested members of the commission by NASA's acting administrator, William R. Graham, who had attended Caltech thirty years earlier and had sat in Physics X, taught by Feynman. Later, he attended Feynman's lectures at Hughes Aircraft. But remarkably, it was Feynman's wife, who had accompanied him to the Hughes lectures, who suggested his name. When Feynman received a phone call from Graham, Feynman told him "You're ruining my life." He meant that he was using his short time because Feynman was battling a rare form of cancer, Waldeström's macroglobulinemia, involving the bone marrow. Feynman refused to consider that the cause of his cancer may have been exposure to radiation during the making of the atomic bomb forty years earlier.

During the investigation, Feynman interviewed a number of NASA engineers and found that there were well-known problems with that rubber O-rings that sealed the joints between sections of the tall solid-fuel rockets. Feynman focused on the cold weather that had caused ice to form on equipment throughout the launchpad. NASA's top space-flight official, Jesse Moore, denied any knowledge that cold could cause any problems.

Another NASA official, Judson A. Lovingwood from the Marshall Space Flight Center in Alabama, mentioned that managers from NASA and Morton Thiokol, builder of the solid rockets, had a telephone conference before the launch where they discussed "a concern by Thiokol on low temperatures." They focused on the O-rings. There was mention of "blow-by"—that is, soot that showed hot gases had burned through one of the O-rings. However, the O-rings were used in pairs, and the second O-ring always held.

A *New York Times* article was published quoting documents with urgent warnings within NASA about the O-rings for at least four years. The warnings stated that failure of the seals could cause "loss of vehicle, mission, and crew to metal erosion, burn-through, and probably cause bursting resulting in fire and deflagration."

General Kutyna, shuttle program manager for the military, had information from engineers and astronauts that Thiokol had known of a potential loss of resiliency when the rubber O-rings were cold.

Feynman was frustrated by inconclusive and evasive testimony. But then, looking at a glass of ice water during dinner, he had an idea. Ice water was at a stable thirty-two degrees Fahrenheit, almost the same temperature at the pad at the time of the launch. He took a taxicab and had it take him to a hardware store where he purchased a C-clamp and pliers. When the hearing began, he asked for a glass of ice water. When a cross-section of the joint was passed for the commissioners to examine, Feynman cut a piece of the O-ring from the model, compressed it with the C-clamp, and put in the ice water. After a break, the chairman of the commission allowed Feynman to make a comment. Feynman took the piece of O-ring from the ice water with the C-clamp and demonstrated that when the material was exposed to a temperature of thirty-two degrees Fahrenheit, it would lose its resilience, and he believed that it had "some significance" for their problem.

A budget analyst, Richard Cook, who had written a memorandum that was quoted in *The New York Times*, was cross-examined by the chairman. The analyst noticed the O-ring problem on a list of "budget threats" month after month and had it highlighted for his superiors. The analyst had described the problem accurately. Feynman's demonstration was on television and newspaper reports that evening and the following morning. Lawrence Mulloy, the project manager for the solid rockets, then admitted that the cold diminished the effectiveness of the seals and NASA had known it. Freeman Dyson said, "The public saw with their own eyes how science is done . . . how nature gives a clear answer when a scientist asks a clear question." The commission, thanks to Feynman's straightforward experiment, had arrived at the physical cause of the accident. Feynman continued his investigation, interviewing engineers from NASA and contractors, and discovered many problems that had been ignored by NASA managers. But politics triumphed, and the final report did not find any NASA manager guilty of negligence and recommended that "NASA continue to receive the support of the Administration and the nation." Feynman's critical comments were isolated in an appendix at the end of the report. He finished his personal report by saying "For a successful technology, reality must take precedence over public relations, for nature cannot be fooled." Feynman died on February 15, 1988. His books, including *The Feynman Lectures*, are still sold in the best bookstores.

Carl Sagan
Adventures in the Cosmos

In 1980, when the PBS series *Cosmos* was running on television, I never missed an episode. By then, I was a first lieutenant in the US Air Force and an intercontinental ballistic missile officer with the Titan II missile system. So I was a rocket man but happy not to have to launch the rocket with a powerful nuclear bomb on top. In 2002, as an instructor of environmental science at the University of Phoenix in Oklahoma City, I would show the video of the episode "Heaven and Hell" where we would travel to Venus in a spaceship of our imagination with Carl Sagan at the controls. Sagan would describe the toxic and extremely hot atmosphere of Venus (hell) with the relative heaven of Earth and talked about the environmentally destructive human activity that threatened to turn Earth into a hell like Venus. At the end of the course, one student wrote, "We want more Carl Sagan!" Most of this chapter came from *Carl Sagan: A Biography*, by Ray Spangenburg and Kit Moser.

Carl Sagan was born in Brooklyn, New York, to a Russian Jewish family. Sagan traced his analytical urges to his mother, Rachel, whose intellectual ambitions were blocked by social restrictions because of her poverty, her being a woman, and her Jewish religion. She worshipped her only son, Carl, who would fulfill her unfulfilled dreams. He attributed his "sense of wonder" to his father, Sam Sagan, an immigrant garment worker. In his book, *Shadows of Forgotten Ancestors*, Sagan describes his parent's influence: "My parents were not scientists. They knew nothing about science. But they taught me the two uneasily cohabiting modes of thought that are central to the scientific method."

He had a sister, Carol Mae (Cari), seven years younger, who was very close to him all his life. In fact, Carl chose her name, as close as possible to his own.

When he was four or five years old, his parents took Carl to the 1939 New York World's Fair. The experience was a turning point in his life, awakening in him a lifelong interest in science and technology. He saw the burial of a time capsule at Flushing Meadows with mementos of the 1930s to be recovered by Earth's descendants in a future millennium. As an adult, Carl Sagan and his colleagues created similar time capsules, but instead of being buried, the capsules were sent out to wander in the vastness of space, to be discovered by extraterrestrial beings.

At the age of five, his mother took him to a public library where he asked the librarian for "a book about the stars." The librarian brought him a book about . . . movie stars! Carl had to explain that he wanted a book about the stars in the sky. And that was the beginning of an intellectual voyage that would last for a lifetime. His parents helped nurture his interest in science by buying him chemistry sets and reading materials. A visit to the Hayden Planetarium at the Museum of Natural History in New York City fed his interest in astronomy. His interest in space was wetted by reading science-fiction stories by Edgar Rice Burroughs such as *A Princess of Mars*, *The Gods of Mars*, and *The Warlord of Mars*. Later, he sent for a book titled *Interplanetary Flight*. This book was not science fiction but was written by the respected British astronomer Arthur C. Clarke and dealt with the possibility of rocket flights to other planets.

Carl entered the University of Chicago at age sixteen in the fall of 1951. Chicago offered the type of broad-based education that a future visionary like him needed. At the time, Chicago required an across-the-board liberal arts education without focusing on any particular academic field until graduate school. He received a bachelor of arts with general and special honors in 1954, a bachelor of science in 1955, and a master of science in physics in 1956 before earning a doctor of philosophy in astronomy and astrophysics in 1960 from the University of Chicago.

During his university years, Sagan developed a disorder known as achalasia, or cardiospasm a condition that interferes with the normal muscle processes that move food through the esophagus to the stomach. Sagan suffered this condition for many years despite efforts by physicians of the Mayo Clinic to correct it. He feared eating, concerned of not being able to swallow. This probably contributed to his thin gawky appearance in his early adult years.

During a visit home, during his freshman year, Carl's mother suggested that he met with the nephew of a friend who was a graduate student of biology at the University of Indiana. Carl and Seymour Abrahamson shared an interest on the origin of life and whether life existed only on Earth on in other parts of the universe. Abrahamson was studying under geneticist Hermann Joseph Muller who had won the Nobel Prize for Physiology or Medicine in 1946 for his work on the genetics of the fruit fly. Muller demonstrated in 1926 that x-rays caused many gene mutations and structural changes in chromosomes. He published his results in 1927 and received the Nobel Prize in 1946. Abrahamson arranged for Sagan and Muller to meet. Muller also shared with them an interest in the origins of life. The Nobelist encouraged Sagan and discussed the possibilities of life in other galaxies, a position rejected at the time by most scientists. Muller invited Sagan to work in his laboratory during summer months between academic years. Sagan enthusiastically accepted. So his friendship with Abrahamson opened for Sagan an opportunity to explore an area of science that physicists rarely explored and, on top of that, to work with a world-class scientist. This was Carl's first experience doing scientific work.

During his summer at Indiana, Sagan developed a strong friendship with Hermann Muller, but he also realized that laboratory work was not for him. He found the job boring and tedious. But Muller was supportive; he listened to Sagan's exploration of ideas and contributed significantly to Sagan's confidence.

Sagan had supreme confidence even as an undergraduate and was not afraid to go to people, regardless of their reputations, and engage them in conversation. He was eloquent and articulate. He spoke with authority and ease, had interesting ideas, and asked good questions. This confidence to deal with famous people earned him several priceless friendships. In addition to working with Muller in 1952, during the summer of 1956, he worked with planetary scientist Gerard Kuiper who, at the time, was the only full-time planetary astronomer in the world. In the summer of 1957, he worked with Nobel Prize–winning physicist George Gamow in Colorado, and in 1959, he worked with Melvin Calvin who would win the Nobel Prize in chemistry in 1961 for his work in photosynthesis. But his most important mentor, who got Sagan accepted in key circles, was geneticist Joshua Lederberg, who shared the Nobel Prize for Physiology or Medicine in 1958 at the young age of thirty-three for his work in genetic structure and function in microorganisms.

The novels of Edgar Rice Burroughs planted in Sagan's mind the seeds for his lifelong yearning to find life in other planets. The discipline that would be known as exobiology and later astrobiology—that is, the study of life as a possibility on other worlds—did not exist at the time Sagan was a student in Chicago. But it was being born right there at Chicago.

In the early 1950s at the University of Chicago, while Sagan was an undergraduate, a graduate student named Stanley Lloyd Miller was working on his PhD under Harold Clayton Urey. Urey won the Nobel Prize for chemistry in 1934 for discovering heavy hydrogen (deuterium), and during WWII, he worked on the Manhattan Project, which developed the atomic bomb. Urey was interested in geochemistry, the formation of planets, and the atmospheric conditions at the beginning of Earth's history. Urey believed that the early Earth's atmosphere was made up of hydrogen-containing gases such as methane (CH_4), ammonia (NH_3), and water vapor (H_2O). An astrophysicist named Cecilia Payne-Gaposhkin, who taught at Harvard in the 1920s, was able to prove that hydrogen is the main ingredient of all stars. She was the first person to earn a PhD in astronomy from either Radcliffe or Harvard (where she took courses). She wrote her dissertation on the composition of the atmosphere of stars. After a while, other astronomers admitted that she was right. It ultimately became clear that hydrogen and helium are the two most abundant elements in the universe—what stars are made of. Because the planets formed from the same nebula that formed the Sun, then logically, the atmosphere of early Earth contained a high concentration of hydrogen.

In 1951, Urey gave a lecture on his theory of the chemical origins of life on Earth and suggested that someone run the experiment. Stanley Miller volunteered. At first, Urey tried to talk him out of it since the experiment was risky and Urey was responsible for Miller to earn a PhD in three years or so. But Miller was determined, and they agreed to try it for six months to a year. If there were no results, then Miller would try something else.

Stanley Miller's experiment is considered a landmark experiment in the history of biology, aimed at simulating the possible early-Earth scenario. He and Urey had postulated that, in early Earth history, great clouds of gases rolled over the surface of the planet and lightning flashed across the skies, jolting molecules of methane, hydrogen, ammonia, and water into various molecular combinations by bolts of lightning. Urey and Miller speculated that inorganic building-block molecules, raining upon Earth's shallow oceans, combined into longer, more complex, organic molecules such as amino acids, proteins, and nucleotides. These molecules would become more and more complex until they eventually would form nucleic acids capable of replicating themselves.

Miller put purified water into a flask carefully sterilized . On top of this water, he created an atmosphere of hydrogen, methane, and ammonia. Then he introduced into this atmosphere an electric charge to simulate lightning. In this scenario, there was no free oxygen but plenty of hydrogen. The results were amazing. In only a couple of days, Miller observed a pinkish-orange substance that was forming. After continuing his experiments for a week, Miller noticed that the water in the flask had turned orange red. After analysis, he found, to his great excitement, that among other substances, he had produced two of the simplest amino acids. And there was indication that other more complex amino acids were forming. His tests found that the water contained a very high concentration of amino acids. After longer trials, more amino acids formed.

Other scientists have successfully repeated the experiment numerous times, producing all twenty protein-forming amino acids. The most amazing thing was that the organic molecules that formed in Miller's apparatus were the same found in living organisms. The experiment did not create living organisms but showed that lightning and the gases involved definitely could initiate a process that produced the chemistry of life. In the late 1960s, more complicated molecules were found in gas clouds in outer space, giving credibility to this theory. Sagan was an undergraduate at Chicago when Miller did his famous experiment. Sagan took a tour in Miller's basement laboratory that Miller called the dungeon. Sagan witnessed the tough questions that Miller endured from other scientists. Some questions were intended to verify that the experiment was conducted properly and without flaws. However, other questions were hostile and emotional. This was a glimpse for Sagan of what he would personally endure years later.

During the 1960s, Sagan would conduct his own experiments, building upon the work of Urey and Miller, but including hydrogen sulfide instead of hydrogen to the mix of gases. He also exposed the mix to ultraviolet radiation, reasoning that early Earth's atmosphere would not have had the ozone layer that now reduces the UV reaching the surface of the earth. And this was Sagan's entry into the field of *exobiology*, a term coined by Nobel laureate Joshua Lederberg to designate the study of life beyond Earth. Regretfully, after all these years, no one has found evidence of life on other worlds. But the success of Miller's experiment showed that under the right circumstances, the building blocks of life could have formed on early Earth. In 1970, Sri Lanka–born biochemist Cyril Ponnamperuma and his team found traces of five amino acids on a meteorite that had landed in Australia on September 28, 1969. Ponnamperuma was able to demonstrate that the meteorite did not pick up these amino acids from contact with Earth. The amino acids were probably synthesized by a process similar to the experiments by Miller and Sagan. Scientists now conclude that the building blocks of life probably originated not on Earth but may have come from outer space, carried by comets and meteorites. Evidence was found by close-up examination of Halley's Comet in 1986 and a spacecraft flyby of some of the moons of Jupiter and other planets that found large quantities of dark organic matter ("goo"). Incredibly, experiments have shown that many complex building blocks of life can survive a meteorite's fiery dive though the Earth's atmosphere.

Sagan and UFOs

As a young man who had been influenced by science-fiction novels, Sagan believed in the possibility of extraterrestrial beings visiting Earth. But as he grew older and wiser, he realized that no one should take at face value every report of an unidentified flying object (UFO) sighting. In 1996, he wrote in *The Demon Haunted World*, "There are no cases—despite well over a million UFO reports since 1947—in which something so strange that it could only be an extraterrestrial spacecraft is reported so reliably that misapprehension, hoax, or hallucination can be reliably excluded." This was a significant shift in the point of view of someone who, as a college student, had written a letter to Dean Acheson, then secretary of state, advising that the government should take precautions in case visitors from outer space were not friendly (I don't know if he ever got a reply from the State Department). He wrote in 1996, "Keeping an open mind is a virtue—but as the space engineer James Oberg once said, not so open that your brains fall out." Eventually, Sagan became a nonbeliever in UFOs. This ability to change his beliefs based on scientific evidence is a sign of a good scientist.

Sagan thought scientists should study UFO reports because there was widespread public interest on the subject. In 1966, Sagan was a member of the Ad Hoc Committee to review Blue Book, the US Air Force's UFO-investigation project. The committee concluded that Blue Book had been lacking as a scientific study and recommended a university-based project that would conduct a scientific study of the UFO phenomenon. The result was the Condon Committee (1966–1968) led by physicist Edward Condon, which concluded that UFOs did not behave in a manner consistent with a threat to national security. At the symposium in 1969 of the American Association for the Advancement of Science (AAAS), Sagan was able to present an event on UFOs where a wide range of educated opinions were offered by a balanced roster of speakers.

Sagan edited the lectures and discussions at the symposium and published them in 1972 as *UFOs: A Scientific Debate*.

In *Cosmos* (1980), Sagan wrote, "There are no compelling cases of extraterrestrial visitation, despite all the claims about UFOs and ancient astronauts that sometimes make it seem that our planet is awash in uninvited guests."

In the summer of 1957, Sagan worked with Dutch-born American astronomer Gerard Peter Kuiper, then director of the McDonald Observatory in Fort Davis, Texas, with McDonald's eighty-two-inch reflector telescope. Kuiper suggested that small bodies orbit the Sun in a belt beyond the orbits of Neptune and Pluto. This region was named the Kuiper Belt in his honor. Kuiper and Sagan shared a curiosity about possible life in other planets. Kuiper had made headlines in newspapers with his hypothesis that lichen-like plant life might be the cause of dark patterns that spread and receded across Mars with the seasons. In the world of science, being famous in newspapers and popular magazines is not approved by colleagues, something that Sagan would soon experience. Kuiper and Sagan could not guess that on October 4, 1957, the Soviets would launch the satellite *Sputnik*, resulting in increased popular interest in space, the creation of NASA, and a space race that would last until the mid-1970s.

Carl and Lynn

Carl met Lynn Alexander at the University of Chicago where she studied biology. Carl was twenty, and Lynn was sixteen, a very attractive and intelligent young woman. Lynn would eventually become Carl's first wife after a turbulent courtship.

Carl and Lynn shared a love of science. But they differed in their views. Carl believed that scientists would ultimately explain life-forms in terms of physics and chemistry. Lynn viewed Earth and all living inhabitants as a single unified organism. In the 1970s, she and a British scientist called James Lovelock developed a Gaia hypothesis (Gaia was the Greek goddess of Earth). Lynn thought that Carl's quest for extraterrestrial life was a silly waste of time. Their philosophical differences would eventually break their relationship.

When Carl headed for the McDonald Observatory in Texas in 1957, Lynn went to Mexico to work in a prestigious anthropology project. Carl visited Lynn in Mexico, but the spicy food aggravated Carl's achalasia, preventing him from eating properly. The constant pain and hunger made Carl bad-tempered during his visit, and he was rude to Lynn's colleagues. An embarrassed and angry Lynn for a time considered not to marry Carl.

Carl and Lynn broke up, got back together, and broke up again and again. To make matters worse, Carl's mother, Rachel, did not like "that scientist." According to Carl's sister Cari, Rachel did not consider any woman to be good enough for Carl. When, during the spring break of 1955, Carl and Lynn visited Princeton, Carl would not introduce Lynn to Rachel, fearing a storm. Lynn visited J. Robert Oppenheimer at the Institute for Advanced Studies in Princeton while Carl visited his family. Even the fact that Lynn was Jewish was not good enough for Rachel.

But eventually, Carl and Lynn got married on June 16, 1957. Lynn received her bachelor's degree a month before the wedding (a liberal arts degree with no declared major). They spent the summer at the University of Colorado at Boulder where Carl rented a house, with a gorgeous view, from a cousin. At Colorado, Lynn studied ecology and plant physiology while Carl studied with the distinguished Russian-American theoretical physicist George Gamow. Gamow had worked on cosmogony (the astrophysical study of the origin and evolution of the universe), radiation, astrophysics, and the theory of the evolutionary universe. This experience was an important intellectual gain for Sagan.

In the fall, Carl returned to his PhD work at Yerkes, and Lynn entered the PhD program in zoology and genetics at the University of Wisconsin at Madison. During the summer of 1958, Lynn became pregnant. Financially, these were tough times for the Sagans. Carl's scholarships had just ended, and he had taken part-time work in Madison. Lynn's fellowship would be on hold until her baby was born. But they managed to muddle through.

Dorion Solomon Sagan was born on March 17, 1959. His first name was part in homage to the novel of Irish-born writer Oscar Wilde *The Picture of Dorian Gray* and part as an allusion to the constellation Orion (D'Orion or "of Orion"). The middle name was after King Solomon, in honor of their Jewish heritage. Dorion would become a science writer and would coauthor several science books with his mother.

During these years, Carl's career was taking off. In 1957, Carl had his first peer-reviewed article, "Radiation and the Origin of the Gene," published in the journal *Evolution.*

In 1956, Carl proposed an alternative to Kuiper's theory about the waning and darkening of vast areas on Mars. Kuiper believed that the changes in shade were caused by lichen-like organisms responding to changes in seasons. Sagan argued that telescopic observations had not found a link between seasons and the changing dark regions. He proposed that giant dust storms could blow across areas of dark lava, covering the areas in darkness. The darkness would disappear when another storm would blow the dust away. The dark areas would appear to regenerate, die off, and regenerate again. There is a principle attributed to a fourteenth-century philosopher called William Occam, which states that the simpler of two possible explanations is closer to the truth. And Sagan's hypothesis was eventually found to be correct.

Another important contribution by Sagan was the explanation for the high temperatures on the surface of Venus. Astronomers had never been able to see the surface of Venus. The planet was thought to be Earth's twin, perhaps with steamy jungles inhabited by creatures. But astronomers knew that there was a lot of carbon dioxide in Venus's atmosphere but no water vapor. Several scientists had different explanations. One explanation was that Venus was bone-dry. Another theory was that all land on Venus was covered with vast oceans. Yet another theory was that Venus was covered with "gooey oceans of petroleum hidden by a cloud cover of smog." In this scenario, in the beginning, Venus's atmosphere had large quantities of hydrocarbons and very little water. Chemical reactions between the carbon in the hydrocarbons and the oxygen in the water vapor produced large quantities of carbon dioxide and depleted the water supply.

Sagan came up with another theory: the greenhouse effect. He knew that scientists had used a radiotelescope on the roof of the Naval Research Laboratory to obtain strong readings from Venus in the microwave region of the electromagnetic spectrum.

This meant that Venus was emitting heat like a microwave oven. They estimated the temperature on the surface of Venus at six hundred degrees Fahrenheit. The scientific community found it hard to accept this news because of the long-held belief that Venus was a planet similar to Earth with living creatures. It was impossible for creatures such as we have on Earth to exist in such a hot environment. In one episode of *Cosmos*, Sagan mentioned one crazy theory that some scientist made: since the planet is covered with thick clouds that will not allow viewing its surface, it was possible that the planet had tropical jungles where dinosaur-like creatures lived. Sagan summarized this theory as "Observation: cant's see a thing; conclusion: dinosaurs!"

Sagan's idea of a greenhouse effect was based on the principle that carbon dioxide, like glass on a greenhouse, allows sunlight from outside to enter but blocks infrared radiation (IR) from escaping. This is what happens when a car sits under the sun. The IR heats the air inside the greenhouse (and the car) until the temperature inside is higher than outside. Sagan knew that carbon dioxide allows frequencies in the IR to pass through. Water vapor also blocks IR from escaping at the frequencies that carbon dioxide missed. Sagan calculated that this combination of carbon dioxide and water vapor would produce a powerful greenhouse effect. The surface of Venus would heat and radiate heat to space. These could be the high temperatures that the scientists at the NRL measured. Spacecraft years later verified that Sagan's theory was true by measuring the surface temperature of Venus at 864 degrees Fahrenheit. It is impossible for life, as we now have on Earth, to exist on Venus.

Sagan and Lederberg

Carl's most important mentor was Joshua Lederberg, who shared the Nobel Prize in Physiology or Medicine in 1958 for his work on the sexual reproduction of bacteria and the transfer and modification of genetic material between bacterium by viruses. Sagan met Lederberg while living in Madison. Both had an interest in the existence of life in other planets. Lederberg coined the term *exobiology* for this concept (today, the term used is *astrobiology*). Lederberg believed that life may not have originated on Earth but may have been carried to Earth from outer space by comets or asteroids, raining down on the Earth's oceans. Sagan and Lederberg exchanged ideas for ten years. Lederberg often defended Sagan's ideas from critics who considered Sagan's thinking as bizarre and off-the-wall. Lederberg coauthored a paper in 1958 with Dean B. Cowie, entitled "Moon Dust," which was published in *Science*. It proposed that layers of frozen dust and organic molecules would have accumulated over billions of years on the surface of the Moon. Astronauts landing on the Moon would bring samples of this organic material to Earth to be studied by biologists. This theory led Lederberg, after the Soviets launched *Sputnik* and started the race to the Moon, to warn against introducing alien biotics from Earth on the Moon and, in turn, bringing biotics from the Moon to Earth. He encouraged concern among members of the National Academy of Sciences (NAS). This concept of planetary contamination was accepted by NASA. The NASA administrator, Hugh Dryden, set up a Space Sciences Board within the NAS with Lederberg heading the exobiology panel of that board. Lederberg suggested that NASA hire Sagan as a part-time researcher and adviser. Sagan's duties would include a review of the literature on subjects to be discussed by the discussion group on the West Coast, prepare their reports for publication, and write a handbook of planetary biology. Sagan's salary was $4,000 per year, which was good for a part-time job in those days. NASA agreed and Sagan, still a graduate student, found himself in the company of Nobel laureates and other scientific luminaries. In 1959, Sagan published an article on planetary contamination in the journal *Science*.

One of the members of the western discussion group was Melvin Calvin, who would win a Nobel Prize in Chemistry in 1961. Calvin invited Sagan to spend the summer of 1959 researching in his lab at the University of California at Berkeley.

Sagan graduated with a PhD in astronomy and astrophysics from the University of Chicago in 1960. His dissertation on "Physical Studies of the Planets" covered several areas that had common life on other planets. One of the topics of his dissertation, "The

Radiation Balance of Venus," had led him to correspond with radio astronomer Frank Drake, which would be an important influence on Sagan's career.

At the end of 1959, Sagan was accepted for the prestigious Miller Fellowship at the University of California at Berkeley. At Berkeley, Sagan would be in the company of famous scientists such as Calvin, Emilio Segre, Luis Alvarez, Glenn Seaborg, Edwin McMillan, and Owen Chamberlain. Lynn was admitted to the graduate program in zoology and genetics at Berkeley. The Sagan family started a chapter of their lives in California.

The USSR launch of *Sputnik* catapulted the role of space exploration as a critical part of the Cold War. There was excellent funding for engineering and science, especially space science. And exobiology was attracting excellent funding. At Berkeley, Sagan had Lederberg across the bay at Stanford, and the two scientists resumed exchanging ideas. Sagan had great interest in exobiology. He also was interested in a project of radio astronomy that involved "listening" for possible messages from civilizations from outer space.

Frank Drake was a radio astronomer working for the National Radio Observatory at Green Bank, West Virginia. Drake attended Cornell University in Ithaca, New York, where he originally planned to major in aeronautical engineering but, instead, studied electronics (or engineering physics as it was called). He was the first student to score 100 percent in the course on basic electronics. He also took a course in astronomy and decided to become an astronomer. In a 1951, Drake attended the Messenger Lectures given by Otto Struve, founder of the McDonald Observatory, who was considered the father of astrophysics. Struve had vast knowledge in the evolution and structure of stars, which he obtained with the use of the spectrograph, an instrument that breaks up light into its components that provide a sort of bar code of information. Struve was able to calculate the speed of a star's spin from the width of its spectral lines since the bar code becomes spread out by the rotation. When a star is spinning, it is coming and going. A star moving away from us appears redder while a star moving closer to us appears bluer. Struve found that the larger stars spin fast while smaller stars (like our Sun) spin slower.

Struve concluded that the fast-spinning stars are lone stars while those spinning slower are impeded by planets. Struve's theory implied that there could be around ninety-nine billion planets in the universe. Struve also announced that it was possible that there would be life in other planets. Astronomers later discovered many other planets, confirming Struve's theory.

Drake graduated with honors from Cornell with a degree in engineering physics and served three years in the US Navy aboard the USS *Albany* as an electronics officer. In 1955, he entered Harvard University to study astronomy. He obtained a summer position at the radio astronomy laboratory, and he became a radio astronomer and eventually earned a PhD from Harvard in radio astronomy in 1958, which at the time was a brand-new science. He soon got a job offer from the new National Radio Astronomy Observatory (NRAO) at Green Banks, West Virginia. NRAO had an eighty-five-foot telescope, at the time the largest radio telescope in existence.

In 1959, with encouragement of the director of NRAO, Drake began work on Project Ozma (named after Princess Ozma in the Oz books). The project would look for radio signals that could be messages from extraterrestrial civilizations. It would be a short project—two weeks long—among other projects of the NRAO. Drake built the receiver so it could be used for other projects after Ozma. Two stars were observed: Tau Ceti and Epsilon Eridani. At the beginning of the search, there was a lot of excitement when a signal was detected; regretfully, it turned out to be a source from Earth. No results were received the rest of the search. But it was a first try, and no one expected to find an extraterrestrial civilization at the first try. Plus it was cheap—it only cost $2,000.

SETI

A year after Ozma, J. Peter Pearman of the Space Science Board contacted Drake with the idea of organizing a conference about the search for extraterrestrial intelligence (SETI). While writing the list of invitees, both Drake and Pearman came up with Sagan's name. Sagan had contacted Drake about a research Drake had done with the eighty-five-foot telescope on the temperature of Venus. Drake and Sagan had continuing correspondence that showed Sagan's interest in exobiology. At twenty-seven, Sagan was the youngest invitee to the conference. During the conference, one participant, Melvin Calvin, got news that he had won the Nobel Prize.

Just before the conference, Frank Drake had devised his now-famous Drake equation as a way to estimate how many intelligent, communicating civilizations might exist in our galaxy. The equation is

$$N = R f_p n_e f_l f_i f_c L$$

Where

N = number of intelligent, communicating civilizations in the Milky Way
R = rate of star formation in the galaxy
f_p = fraction of those stars that have planets
n_e = number of environmentally appropriate planets orbiting those stars
f_l = fraction of planets with life
f_i = fraction of planets with intelligent life
f_c = fraction of intelligent life–bearing planets that can send communication
L = fraction of planet's life that a communicating civilization may survive

During the conference, Sagan and the other attendees tried to come with reasonable estimates for these variables. Of course, each scientist had his own estimates. The equation is a good tool to stimulate thinking, but there is no way, at this time, to obtain an accurate result.

Today, Frank Drake heads the SETI Institute in Mountain View, California, founded in 1984 and is involved in the Carl Sagan Center for the Study of Life in the Universe.

On May 25, 1961, President John F. Kennedy announced the intention to land American astronauts on the Moon by the end of the decade.

The Mariner Missions

In 1962, NASA's Jet Propulsion Laboratory (JPL) launched two missions to the planet Venus. *Mariner 1*, launched on July 22, 1962, malfunctioned and had to be destroyed shortly after takeoff. But *Mariner 2*, launched in August 1962, was a success. Sagan was part of the Mariner science team. This was the beginning of a career of consulting for NASA's JPL. JPL, at Pasadena, California, managed by the California Institute of Technology (Caltech), would become the heart of NASA's planetary exploration program.

Sagan published his article "The Planet Venus" in *Science*. In the article, Sagan explained his hypothesis that a greenhouse effect on Venus was responsible for the extremely high temperatures measured by scientists using Earth-based instruments. Sagan risked being proven wrong when *Mariner 2* flew close to Venus. But on December 14, 1962, *Mariner 2* flew by Venus, scanning the planet with its radiometers, revealing that Venus has cool dust clouds and an extremely hot surface. Carl's interpretation that Venus had an extremely hot surface was proven correct. His theory of the greenhouse effect, although not proven, w

The publication of his article in *Science* attracted the attention of Harvard University. Two top Harvard astronomers—Fred Whipple, who headed the Astronomy Department, and Donald Menzel, a specialist in solar studies—contacted Sagan to lead a colloquium at Harvard. The colloquium was such a success due to Sagan's abilities as an orator that Whipple and Menzel convinced the school to offer Sagan a position as a lecturer on the astronomy faculty and a joint post at the Smithsonian Astrophysical Observatory. Any young PhD would have jumped at the opportunity. But Sagan played it cool and demanded that the position be upgraded to assistant professor, and surprisingly, Harvard agreed.

In 1962, Lynn told Carl that she and their two children, Dorion (then three) and Jeremy (two) were leaving him and she was filing for divorce. Carl tried to talk her out of it but Lynn was determined. Carl did not realize that his commitment to his career had caused this problem. Lynn complained that he was never home; he did not help her with the household, raising the children, or handling the finances. She had no time for her PhD. On the other hand, Lynn thought that Carl's interest in extraterrestrial life was silly and a waste of time. This basic incompatibility was also an underlying cause for the divorce. Carl's mother had raised him as the focus of attention, not with attention to cooperation or compromise. Their divorce was finalized in 1963.

Lynn completed her PhD in genetics at UC Berkeley in 1965. She was married to crystallographer Thomas Margulis from 1967 to 1980 and changed her name to Lynn Margulis. She was on the faculty of Boston University from 1966 to 1988. She wrote *Origin of Eukaryotic Cells* while at Boston. Since 1988, Lynn has been a full professor at the University of Massachusetts where she now holds the title of distinguished university professor in the Department of Geosciences. Between 1970 and 2002, she wrote eight books (four with her son Dorion, a science writer, between 1986 and 1995). In 1983, she was elected to the National Academy of Sciences, and in 1999, she was awarded the Presidential Medal of Science by President William J. Clinton.

After nearly five years at Harvard, Sagan was assured by his department head, Fred Whipple, that there should be no problem with being awarded tenure and a secure future at Harvard. But then to everyone's surprise, Sagan was denied tenure. There has been a lot of conjecture about the cause for this. One theory is that his colleagues had become jealous of his fame. Another is that Carl's ideas on extraterrestrial life were too "brash" for Harvard's conservatism. Another more probable cause was that Harold Urey (Nobel Prize in Chemistry, 1934) was asked for a recommendation by Harvard, and he wrote a very unfavorable response. Urey was concerned that Sagan's work was trivial and not good science. Because of this letter, Sagan was not hired at MIT when he applied afterward (Urey apologized to Sagan years later). Sagan was eventually hired as director of the Laboratory for Planetary Studies at Cornell University at Ithaca, New York, in 1968. Cornell was the right choice for Sagan. Sagan fit perfectly at Ithaca. The atmosphere at Ithaca was looser than the stolid atmosphere at Harvard. At Harvard, Sagan was considered eccentric; at Cornell, he was a star.

Carl met Linda Saltzman, an art student in Boston, after his divorce from Lynn. When the time came for Carl to move to

Ithaca, Linda advised him that if he wanted her to go with him, they had to be married. And they were married on April 6, 1968.

On July 20, 1969, the Apollo 11 astronauts, Neil Armstrong and Buzz Aldrin, landed on the Moon. Carl watched on TV under the effects of painkillers after complications of surgery of his esophagus (to make swallowing easier). That resulted in a collapsed lung and the lung cavity filling with blood. Carl survived, but his achalasia continued to plague him the rest of his life.

The Plaque of Pioneer 10 and 11

In December 1969, Eric Burgess of the Christian Science Monitor and Richard Hoagland, planetarium lecturer, proposed an idea that they knew Sagan would love. A spacecraft named *Pioneer 10* would be sent to a journey into the cosmos. It would leave Earth and fly by Jupiter, taking measurements of its magnetic field. Then using Jupiter's gravitational pull, it would speed off and eventually leave our solar system to journey forever through interstellar space. Burgess and Hoagland proposed to send a physical message to whoever was beyond our solar system. Carl checked with NASA to see if the agency would agree to affix a message to the spacecraft, and NASA agreed. Sagan and Frank Drake discussed the type of message to be sent.

The area available would be six inches by nine inches on a metal plate. They decided to do a line drawing with a galactic map showing the spacecraft traveling from Earth and leaving the solar system between Jupiter and Saturn. There would be also a nude man and woman on a side view of the spacecraft. The man has his right hand raised as a greeting. The diagrams would also show the position of the solar system in the galaxy using a pulsar (an object in space that emits radio waves) to show the historical time and place of the launch. There would also be a diagram of the hydrogen atom, the most common element in the universe. Carl's second wife, Linda Saltzman, an artist, was asked to do the drawings. Linda blended the features of the man and the woman to try not to have them resemble Caucasian, Asiatic, or Negroid. When the drawings were finished, they were etched on a gold-anodized aluminum plaque.

On March 2, 1972, *Pioneer 10* was launched. Regretfully, there was a loud outcry about the plaque. Feminist groups objected that the man had his arm raised, making the woman look subservient. Other groups thought the figures looked blond (line drawings on a gold plaque; no way to avoid that). Many people did not like the fact that the two figures were nude and considered it immoral. Can't satisfy everybody! All we can do is wait to see if extraterrestrial beings find the craft and find out what their reaction will be.

During this period, in September 1970, Linda gave birth to a son, Julian Zapata Sagan, and also in 1970, Carl was promoted to full professor of astronomy at Cornell. Also, he began working at JPL's Viking mission to Mars.

In 1973, Sagan published his first book, *The Cosmic Connection: An Extraterrestrial Perspective*—a celebration of the cosmos. This book was the idea of entrepreneur Jerome Agel who contacted Sagan and proposed the idea to him. By this time, people were distracted by other issues such as the Vietnam War and anti-war riots. Sagan and Agel were rejected by seventeen publishers before finally landing a contract with Doubleday. Sagan wrote a series of short essays in his easygoing and personable style on a wide range of topics. In addition to writing about life in other planets and the intelligence of dolphins, Sagan also debunked some pseudoscience ideas, such as myths and legends about visitations to Earth made by extraterrestrial spacecraft. The book became a best seller.

One defining moment in Sagan's career was an appearance on Johnny Carson's *The Tonight Show*. Carson saw Sagan's appearance on Dick Cavett's program and invited him to appear on his show. His first appearance was on November 30, 1973, and was a roaring success. Sagan's relaxed demeanor, not wearing a business suit or glasses, and not giving himself airs of intellectual superiority definitely contributed to the show's great success. Thus began a twenty-year relationship between Johnny Carson and Carl Sagan. On March 24, 1974, Sagan appeared in a program of the Public Broadcasting System's *NOVA* called "The Search for Life." An article in TV Guide about the program was read by ten million people. On July 15, 1974, *Time* magazine included Sagan among the two hundred "rising leaders" of young adults.

In 1973, Timothy Ferris, who was a science journalist and New York Bureau chief of *Rolling Stone* magazine, had the great idea to interview Sagan. The article appeared on June 7, 1973, and helped promote Sagan's image as a popular scientist. Sagan and Ferris became friends, and Sagan wrote the introduction to Ferris's book on astronomy, *The Red Limit: The Search for the Edge of the Universe*, published in 1977. At a dinner party where Sagan and Ferris were invited in 1974, Ferris brought his girlfriend, writer Ann Druyan. Druyan had majored in literature at New York University. Sagan and Druyan became friends, and years later, Druyan would become Sagan's third wife.

The Arecibo Message

In November 1974, Sagan and Frank Drake conducted a project that they had been planning since 1971: use the world's largest radio telescope near the city of Arecibo, Puerto Rico, to do a search for extraterrestrial intelligence (SETI) of nearby galaxies. They also sent a now-famous message to star cluster M13.

The official name of the Arecibo Observatory is the National Astronomy and Ionosphere Center. Construction began the summer of 1960 and officially opened on November 1, 1963. It is operated by Cornell University under cooperative agreement with the National Science Foundation. The observatory has a spherical reflector with a 1,001-foot diameter, built inside the depression left by a karst sinkhole. Karst formations are limestone mountains formed when mildly acidic water dissolves bedrock such as limestone or dolostone. The giant size of the reflector is the largest curved focusing antenna on the planet, making it the world's most sensitive radio telescope.

In November 1974, the Arecibo observatory had just received a major upgrade. The equipment at Arecibo allowed for scanning hundreds of billions of stars at one time. The new multichannel receivers could pick up a thousand channels at once.

On November 16, 1974, a message was broadcast into space a single time via frequency-modulated radio waves, aimed at the globular star cluster M13, some 25,000 light years away. The message consisted of 1,679 binary digits, approximately 210 bytes. The total broadcast was less than 3 minutes. The number 1679 was chosen because it is the product of two prime numbers, to be arranged rectangularly as 73 rows by 23 columns. The alternative, 23 rows by 73 columns, produces jumbled nonsense. Frank Drake wrote the message, assisted by Sagan, among others. The message consisted of seven parts:

1. The numbers one through ten
2. The atomic numbers of the elements hydrogen, carbon, nitrogen, oxygen, and phosphorous, which make up the deoxyribonucleic acid (DNA) molecule
3. The formulas for the sugars and bases in DNA
4. The number of nucleotides in DNA and a graphic of the double helix structure of DNA
5. A graphic figure of a human, the physical height of an average man, and the human population of Earth
6. A graphic of the solar system
7. A graphic of the Arecibo radio telescope and the physical diameter of the transmitting antenna dish

The message will take 25,000 years to reach its destination and another 25,000 years for a reply to return to Earth. The message was more a demonstration of human technological achievement than any attempt to establish a conversation with an extraterrestrial civilization. On top of that, the stars of M13 will not be in the location they were in November 1974 when the message arrives. On November 12, 1999, a Cornell news press release explained that the real purpose of the message was to demonstrate the capabilities of the Arecibo equipment, not to make contact.

Viking: Search for Life on Mars

NASA sent several successful missions to Mars—*Mariner 4, 6, 7*, and *9*. *Mariner 4* arrived at Mars on July 14, 1965, and reported that there were no radiation belts and no magnetic field. But what made *Mariner 4* different was it carried cameras. To Sagan's—and all of our—disappointment, the photos showed no sign of life: no canals, no vegetation, and no water, only a rust-colored barren waste. Mars was as lifeless as our Moon.

Mariner 9 entered orbit around Mars, rather than flying by. It was the first artificial satellite of a planet other than Earth where it took over seven thousand photos of the planet's surface. Among other things, *Mariner 9* photographed large regions that showed that large floodwaters and rivers may have flowed in the past.

The Viking 1 and 2 missions in the mid-1970s were no luckier as far as life on Mars. *Viking 1* landed on Mars on July 20, 1976. Again, no sign of life. Sagan said, "There was not a hint of life, no bushes, no trees, no cactus, no giraffes, antelopes or rabbits." After much debate among Sagan and other scientists, the decision was made to land *Viking 2* up north, and on September 3, 1976, *Viking 2* landed at Utopia Planitia (Plains of Utopia).

Each Viking lander carried three biology experiments to search for life on Mars. They discovered some unexplained activity in the soil. But no microorganisms were detected at either site. Biologists concluded that the Martian surface self sterilized. Environmental factors such as harsh UV radiation from the Sun, the soil's extreme dryness, and the oxidizing process in the soil prevented life to exist on Mars. A fourth experiment on board the Vikings was a gas chromatograph and mass spectrometer on both landers, but they found no sign of organic chemistry. X-ray fluorescence spectrometers measured elements in the Martian soil. The two Viking landers were the last missions to land successfully on Mars for twenty years, until 1997.

In 1976, Sagan was appointed to the David Duncan Chair as professor of astronomy and space sciences at Cornell University. His extracurricular activities were bringing prestige and stature to his institution. But his marriage to Linda was starting to fall apart. Linda also complained that he was never home, and his job took priority over his family. She also complained that Carl left all the household and child-raising work to her and had no concern for her career.

In 1977, Sagan published *The Dragons of Eden* on the evolution of human intelligence. This book won the Pulitzer Prize in 1978 for general nonfiction.

Voyager

In 1977, a pair of spacecraft, *Voyager 1* and *Voyager 2*, was launched. Their primary mission was exploration of Jupiter and Saturn. *Voyager 2*'s mission was later extended to explore Uranus and Neptune. Afterward, the spacecraft were to leave the solar system and fly into outer space. Both spacecraft are now (2011) in the heliosheath—the outermost layer of heliosphere where the solar wind is slowed by the pressure of interstellar gas.

After the precedent of the metal plaques carried by *Pioneers 10* and *11*, NASA decided to send a more ambitious message with the Voyager spacecraft to communicate information about our world to extraterrestrials. The Voyager message is contained in phonograph records (a twelve-inch gold-plated copper disk) containing sounds and images to show the diversity and culture on Earth. A committee chaired by Sagan selected the contents of the records—one hundred fifteen images and a variety of natural sounds, including those made by surf, wind and thunder, birds, whales, and other animals. There are also musical selections from different cultures and eras and spoken greetings in fifty-five languages. Linda had the task of assembling the greetings. The greetings begin with Akkadian, spoken in Sumer six thousand years ago, and end with Wu, a modern Chinese dialect. There were also printed messages from President Jimmy Carter and UN Secretary General Waldheim. Following the section of the sounds of Earth, there is a ninety-minute section of music of Eastern and Western classics and ethnic music.

By 1990, the Voyagers were beyond the orbit of Pluto. It will be forty thousand years before they approach any other planetary system. If there are any advanced spacefaring civilizations in interstellar space, the spacecraft may be encountered and the records played.

In February 1990, Sagan convinced NASA to have *Voyager 1*, as it was passing Saturn, to take a picture of Earth from 3.7 billion miles away. As he wrote in *The Pale Blue Dot*, Earth was "just a point of light, a lovely, pixel, hardly distinguishable from the many other points of light Voyager could see."

Cosmos

The Viking missions had the public's interest first hot with the expectation of finding life on Mars and then cold when no life was found. The NASA scientists felt rebuffed. Sagan realized that the scientists had made no effort to communicate to the public their findings in a language the public could understand.

Gentry Lee, the Viking data analysis and mission planning director, proposed to Sagan that both of them should create a production company for communicating science. Sagan liked the idea, but he was no lover of television, which he considered to have low standards for science. However, Sagan admired the popular TV series *Ascent of Man* narrated by Jacob Bronowski. When KCET-TV, a PBS station in Los Angeles, contacted him about doing a TV series on science that would parallel *Ascent of Man*, Sagan agreed. Sagan and Lee agreed to do a thirteen-episode program to air in the fall of 1980. Originally, Sagan planned to call it *Man and the Cosmos*, but Ann Druyan convinced him the title sounded sexist, and he changed it to *Cosmos*.

The series was written by Sagan, Ann Druyan, and Cornell astronomer Steven Soter. Lee and Sagan hired British director Adrian Malone who was the director and cowriter of the *Ascent of Man* series. Malone was used to having free reins, and Sagan wanted control. The two men clashed quickly and, at times, would not talk to each other. But *Cosmos: A Personal Voyage* was made. The series, first broadcasted by the Public Broadcasting Service in 1980, became the most widely watched series in the history of American public television (until *Civil War* in 1990). As of 2009, it was still the most widely watched series in the world. It won an Emmy and a Peabody Award and has been broadcast in more than sixty countries and seen by over a billion people worldwide. A book, *Cosmos*, to accompany the series, was published in 1980, and it rose to the top of the *New York Times* best-seller list for seventy weeks!

Carl's father, Sam Sagan, died of lung cancer in 1979, a year before the first episode of *Cosmos* aired. In his novel (later a movie), *Contact*, Sagan wrote about a SETI scientist named Ellie Arroway who travels to another planet and visits an alien civilization. She

A Few Great Scientists

meets with a representative who has taken the shape of her dead father. This episode reveals Sagan's grief over the death of his own father.

The popularity of *Cosmos* made Sagan a pop star among the young. Recently, his son, Dorion Sagan, wrote in an essay entitled "My Father":

> My father's work made science cool. He showed that it was good to be smart, to be open to wonder but also critical, both of superstition and political authority. The universe was our home. Space exploration and evolution were part of a story based on evidence that belonged to all humanity, not to a religious or political elite looking out for their own interests . . . He showed not only that science belonged to everybody, but that a scientifically educated public was necessary for the health of society. In short, he used television to democratize the advances of the Renaissance and Enlightenment.

In May 1981, Sagan's divorce from Linda became final, and Carl and Annie married on June 1 of that year. Ann and Carl complemented each other. They worked together on writing projects. Carl became more relaxed and more willing to listen to the views of others.

Nuclear Winter

For years during the Cold War, Sagan was concerned about the effects of a nuclear war. He thought that the silence during SETI searches was related to the L in Drake's equation—that is, technically advanced civilizations had destroyed themselves. In the 1980s, Sagan and other scientists became concerned about the effect of nuclear blasts on the climate where widespread ash and smoke thrown into the atmosphere would remain suspended for a year or more, blocking out sunlight, killing plants and other forms of life, and causing a global ice age. Carl coined the phrase "nuclear winter." He and other scientists R. P. Turco, O. B. Toon, T. P. Ackerman, and J. B. Pollack developed the concept of nuclear winter and published the TTAPS report (using the first letter of the last name of each author, with the *S* for Sagan). This theory is still controversial today. But the idea sprang from the theory of the extinction of the dinosaurs, proposed by the father-and-son team of Luis and Walter Alvarez. Walter Alvarez, a geologist, found a mysterious substance while digging a layer of rock that was sixty-five million years old. He consulted his father, Nobel-laureate physicist (and one of the leading scientists who developed the atomic bomb during World War II) Luis Alvarez. Luis found that the substance was radioactive iridium, a substance common in space but not on the surface of the Earth. This was additional evidence that dinosaurs were killed by the impact of a large asteroid that fell in the Yucatan Peninsula in Mexico. The collision ignited fires, and the ash dispersed through the atmosphere, causing an ice age that destroyed the dinosaurs and most living creatures on Earth. Sagan saw a parallel between this scenario and the effects of a global thermonuclear war. In his 1983 article, "Nuclear Winter," Sagan wrote,

> There are now more than 50,000 nuclear weapons, more than 13,000 megatons of yield, deployed in the arsenals of the United States and the Soviet Union—enough to obliterate a million Hiroshimas.
>
> Likewise, in 1973, it was discovered that high-yield airbursts will chemically burn the nitrogen in upper air, converting it into oxides of nitrogen; these, in turn, combine with and destroy the protective ozone layer in the Earth's stratosphere. The surface of the Earth is shielded from deadly solar ultraviolet radiation by a layer of ozone so tenuous that, were it brought down to sea level, it would be only 3 millimeters thick. Partial destruction of this ozone layer can have serious consequences for the biology of the entire planet.

When the US *Mariner 9* spacecraft arrived at Mars, it was noted that the planet was enveloped by a global dust storm. When the dust particles fell to the surface, changes in atmospheric temperature were measured. Sagan and his colleagues studied the cooling effects of dust aerosols from volcanic explosions on Earth. The results of their mathematical model were in good accord with temperature changes measured. Then they applied the mathematical model to the effects of a nuclear war. They calculated the effect from groundbursts (at hardened missile silos, for example) and airbursts (over cities and unhardened military installations) and found that land temperatures could drop up to -25 degrees Celsius (-13 degrees Fahrenheit) and would stay below freezing for months—even for a summer war.

Sagan and his colleagues considered the effects of a limited nuclear war—that is, where no more than one hundred megatons were exploded (less than 1 percent of the world's arsenal in 1983). And only in low yield airbursts over cities. (In an airburst, the fire ball does not reach the ground, preventing the formation of radioactive fallout. The US nuclear doctrine in the 1980s called for airbursts).

The findings by Sagan and his colleagues received support from a report by the US National Research Council in December 1984. In 1985, the US Department of Defense acknowledged the validity of this research but announced that it would not make any change in US defense policies. Now let me add some of my knowledge as a former US Air Force intercontinental ballistic missile (ICBM) officer. The motto of the USAF Strategic Air Command, which controlled all American nuclear-armed bombers and land-based ICBMs during the Cold War, was Peace Is Our Profession. The idea was not to start a nuclear war against the Soviet Union or the People's Republic of China but to deter them from launching a nuclear attack against us. In this sense, Sagan's article on nuclear winter actually helped the United States and its allies in the North Atlantic Treaty Organization (NATO) to deter nuclear war. So Sagan became, in my view, a reluctant "nuclear warrior" although he and Ann were arrested in 1987 while protesting at the Nevada test site where the federal government tests underground nuclear bombs.

Since the end of the Soviet Union and the Cold War, the issue of nuclear winter has lost the public's attention. Some may argue that the proliferation of nuclear weapons among developing countries makes the likelihood of nuclear war greater. We need to remind the nuclear countries of the twenty-first century of the risk of nuclear winter to continue to deter a nuclear exchange.

Carl's Death

In late 1994, Ann noticed a large bruise on Carl's arm that would not heal and asked him to see a doctor. The doctor did a test, and Carl went on a trip to Houston. While Carl was in Houston, the doctor called Ann, wanting Carl to return for a retest. He said there must be a laboratory error because the lab results were for a very sick person. Regretfully, the results were accurate and Carl was diagnosed with myelodysplasia, a bone-marrow disease also called smoldering leukemia. Carl kept working and published a book called *The Demon-Haunted World* where he wrote a list of mistakes he had made in his career. This would be the last book he published during his lifetime. A bone-marrow transplant, with bone marrow donated by his sister Cari, failed to save Carl's life.

Carl died of pneumonia at the age of sixty-two at the Fred Hutchinson Cancer Research Center in Seattle, Washington, on December 20, 1996. He was buried at Lakeview Cemetery in Ithaca, New York. In 1997, the movie *Contact*, based on Carl's novel, was released—starring Jodie Foster as SETI scientist Ellie Arroway—to great popular success. At the end of the film, the words "For Carl" flashed upon the screen, bringing tears to the eyes of many viewers.

Reference List

Alfred Nobel: The King of Dynamite

Fant, Kenne, 1991, *Alfred Nobel A Biography*, Arcade Publishing, New York

Alfred Nobel. (2008, November 29). New World Encyclopedia, Retrieved Marcxh 5, 2011 from http://www.newworldencyclopedia.org/entry/Alfred_Nobel

Alfred Nobel-His Life and Work. Nobel Prize.org. Retrieved April 11, 1010, from http://nobelprize.org/cgi-bin/print?from=%2Falfred_nobel%2Fbiographical%2Farticles%2

Ascanio Sobrero. Answers.com. Retrieved on April 24, 2011 from http://www.answers.com/topic/ascanio-sobrero

Jie Jack Li, Laughing Gas, Viagra and Lipitor: the Human Stories Behind the Drugs we Use. Oxford University Press, 2006. Pages 79-80

The Nobel Peace Prize 1905, Bertha von Suttner. Nobel Lectures, Peace 1901-1925, Editor Frederick W. Haberman, Elsevier Publishing Company, Amsterdam, 1972. Retrieved from http://nobelprize.org/nobel_prizes/peace/laureates/1905/suttner.html?print+1

Branobel. Retrieved on May 22, 2011 from http://en.wikipedia.org/wiki/Branobel

Abrahams, Irwin; "Where there's a Will...The Struggle Over Alfred Nobel's Testament"; http://www.irwinabrams.com/articles/will.html

"Excerpt from the Will of Alfred Nobel". Nobelprize.org. 4 Jul 2011 http://nobelprize.org/alfred_nobel/will/short_testamente.html.

"Ragnar Sohlman". Nobelprize.org. 4 Jul 2011 http://nobelprize.org/alfred_nobel/biographical/articles/life-work/sohlman.html.

"Alfred Nobel and His Interest in Literature". Nobelprize.org 4 Jul 2011

http://nobelprize.org/alfred_nobel/biographical/articles/erlandsson/index.html.
Arendt, Paul; "Nobel's raunchy anti-capitalist play gets world premiere".
http://www.guardian.co.uk/culture/2005/sep/08/threatre.nobelprize2005/print
Building the Bofors guns at Chrysler Corporation: challenges and accomplishments, http://www.allpar.com/history/military/bofors.html

Bofors 40 mm, http://en.wikipedia.org/wiki/Bofors_40_mm, retrieved from the world wide web on 7/22/2011

John von Neumann: Mathematical Genius

Macrae, Norman. *John von Neumann*. New York:P Pantheon Books, 1992.

Rhodes, Richard. *The Making of the Atomic Bomb*. New York: Touchtone, 1986.

Kunkle, Daniel. John von Neumann: Genius of Man and Machine, retrieved on 4/24/2011 from www.redfish.com/dkunkle/vonNeumann

John von Neumann (1903-1957), retrieved on 4/24/2011 from www.atomicarchive.com/Bios/vonNeumann.shtml

Von Neumann, John: 1903-1957, retrieved on 4/24/2011 from www.light-science.com/vonneumann.html

Order of magnitude, http://www.answers.com/topic/orders-of-magnitude

John Presper Eckert, www.bookrags.com, retrieved from the world wide net on September 11, 2011

John Mauchly, http://en.wikipedia.org/wiki/John_Mauchly, retrieved from the world wide net on September 11, 2011

Klaus Fuchs (19111-1988), www.atomic archive.com/Bios/Fuchs.shtml, retrieved from the internet on 10/16/2011

Boyne, Walter J. *A History of U.S. Air Force 1947-1997*. New York: St. Martin's Press, 1997.

Marina von Neumann Whitman, http//en.wikipedia.org/wiki/Marina_von_Neumann_Whitman, retrieved from the world wide web on 12/04/2011

Watson, and Crick: The Search for the Double Helix

Watson, James D., 1996 [orig. 1968], The *Double Helix: A personal Account of the discovery of the structure of DNA*, Scribner, New York

Watson, James D., 2007, *Avoid Boring People*, Alfred A. Knopf, New York
http://en.wikipedia.org/wiki/James_D._Watson

James D. Watson Biography, *From Nobel Lectures, Physiology or Medicine 1942-1962*, Elsevier Publishing Company, Amsterdam, 1964

http://en.wikipedia.org/wiki/Francis_Crick
Francis Crick Biography, From Nobel Lectures, Physiology or Medicine 1942-1962, Elsevier Publishing Company, Amsterdam, 1964
http://en.wikipedia.org/wiki/Maurice_Wilkins
Maurice Wilkins Biography, From Nobel Lectures, Physiology or Medicine 1942-1962, Elsevier Publishing Company, Amsterdam, 1964
www.sdsc.edu/ScienceWomen/franklin.html, Rosalind Elsie Franklin Pioneer Molecular Biologist
Erwin Chargaff, Austrian-American biochemist, http://www.answers.com/topic/erwin-chargaff?&print=true
The famous paper by Watson and Crick, "A Structure for Deoxyribose Nucleic Acid" published in Nature on April 25, 1953 as well as the papers published in the same issue of Nature by Maurice Wilkins "Molecular Structure of Deoxyentose Nucleic Acids" and the paper by Rosalind Franklin "Molecular Configuration in Sodium Thymonucleate" are available at http://www.nature.com/nature/dna50/archive.htm

Norman Borlaug and his army of hunger fighters

Hesser, Leon, 2006, *The Man Who Fed the World and His Battle to End World Hunger, Durban House, Dallas*
Les Prix Nobel en 1970, Editor Wilhem Odelber, [Nobel Foundation], 1971, Norman Borlaug Nobel Prize Acceptance Speech
Biography: Norman Borlaug Ending World Hunger, http://www.achievement.org/autodoc/printmember/bor0bio-1
http://www.rockefellerfoundation.org/who-we-are/our-history
A Timeline of Dr. Norman Borlaug's Work Involving the Rockefeller Foundation, www.rockefellerfoundation.org
http://nobelprize.org/nobel_prizes/peace/laureates/1970/press.html, "The Nobel Peace Prize 1970-Presentation Speech". Nobelprize.org
The Life of Norman Borlaug, 2005, AgBioworld, www.agbioworld.org/biotech-info/topics/life-of-borlaug
Avery, Dennis T., Norman Borlaug is the Greatest Living American, The Steward (Hawaii), January 21, 2006
Borlaug, Norman; May 13, 2002, We Can Feed The World. Here's How, Wall Street Journal
Okoko, Tervil, June 7, 2000, Norman Borlaug Blasts GMO Doomsayers, Africa News Service

Biotechnology Origin, Definition and Old Vs New Biotechnology, www.molecular-plant-biotechnology.info
History of Biotechnology, http:en.wikipedia.org/wiki/History_of_biotechnology
Borkowski, Liz, "Are More Food Crises on the Way?, http://scienceblogs.com/thepumphandle

Jonas Salk: The man who conquered Polio

Sherrow, Victoria, 2008, *Jonas Salk: Beyond the Microscope*, Chelsea House Publishers, New York
http://www.pbs.org, 1998, A Science Odyssey: People and Discoveries: Jonas Salk
http://www.achievement.org
iography: Jonas Salk Developer of Polio Vaccine, Academy of Achievement, 2005
http://www.accessexcellence.org, Okonek, B and Morganstein, L, Development of Polio Vaccines, Access Excellence Classic Collection
Polioforever's Blog; http://polioforever.wordpress.com/jonas-salk

Rachel Carson and the birth of the environmental movement

Linda Lear and J.E. de Steiguer are my main sources for this chapter.
Carson, Rachel, 1962, Silent Spring, Houghton, Miffling Company, New York
Lear, Linda; Rachel Carson: Witness for Nature; Mariner Books, New York, 1997
Lear, Linda; Rachel Louise Carson, www.rachelcarson.org/pages/bio.aspx, retrieved from the world wide web on 12/29/2011
Steiguer, J. E., 1997, The Age of Environmentalism, McGraw-Hill, Boston, Massachusetts, pages 29-41
US Fish and Wildlife Service; Rachel Carson (1907-1964), www.fws.nortyheast/carson/carsonbio, retrieved from the worldwide web on 12/18/2011
Wright, Richard and Nebel, Bernard, *Environmental Science*, 8th edition, Prentice-Hall, Inc., 2003

Richard Feynman: Physicist, Genius, and a Very Funny Curious Character

Feynman, Richard, Surely You're Joking, Mr. Feynman!, W.W. Norton & Company, New York, 1985
Gleick, James, Genius, Vintage Books, New York, 1993

Rhodes, Richard, The Making of the Atomic Bomb, Touchtone, New York, 1986
"Richard P. Feynman - Biographical". Nobelprize.org. Nobel Media AB 2013. Web. 16 Oct 2013.
"Nobel Prize in Physics 1965 - Presentation Speech". Nobelprize.org. Nobel Media AB 2013. Web. 16 Oct 2013.

Carl Sagan: Adventures in the Cosmos

Ray Sprangenburg & Kit Moser, *Carl Sagan: A Biography*, Prometheus Books, 2009 (this was my principal source for this chapter)
"Carl Sagan", http://en. Wikipedia.org/wiki/Carl_Sagan, 2010
"Frank Drake", http//en.wikipedia.org/wiki/Frank_Drake, 2011
"Arecibo Message", http://en.wikipedia.org/wiki/Arecibo_message, 2010
"Arecibo Observatory", http://en.wikipedia.org/wiki/recibo_Observatory
"The 305 meter Radio Telescope", http://www.naic.edu/public/the_telescope.htm
"Karst", http://en.wikipedia.org/wiki/Kast
Carl Sagan, *Cosmos*, Random House Publishing Group, 1980
Carl Sagan, "Nuclear Winter", 1983, http://www.cooperativeindividualism.org/sagan_nuclear_winter.html
"Carl Sagan Center for the Study of Life in the Universe", http:www.seti-inst.edu/csc/index.php
Carl Sagan, *Pale Blue Dot: A Vision of the Human Future in Space*, Random House Publishing Group, 1994
Carl Sagan, Edited by Ann Druyan, *The Varieties of Scientific Experience: A Personal View of the Search for God*, The Penguin Press, New York, 2006
Dorian Sagan, "My Father", http:// kepler.nasa.gov/education/sagan/DorianSaganEssay, 2010
"Mariner 2", http//en.wikipedia.org/wiki/Mariner_2
"Pioneer 10", hppt://www.aerospace guide.net/pioneer11110.html
"Voyager", http://voyager.jpl.nasa.gov

CPSIA information can be obtained
at www.ICGtesting.com
Printed in the USA
FFOW03n1808020817
38385FF